Everything You Know About Planet Earth is Wrong

Dedication: To Christine and Trevor.

First published in the United Kingdom in 2018 by Batsford
43 Great Ormond Street
London WC1N 3HZ
An imprint of Pavilion Books Company Ltd

Copyright © Batsford, 2018
Text copyright © Matt Brown, 2018
Illustrations by Sara Mulvanny

ISBN: 9781849944540

A CIP catalogue record for this book is available from
the British Library.

25 24 23 22 21 20 19 18
10 9 8 7 6 5 4 3 2 1

Reproduction by Mission Productions, Hong Kong
Printed and bound by Imak Ofset, Turkey

This book can be ordered direct from the publisher at the
website www.pavilionbooks.com, or try your local bookshop.

Distributed in the United States and Canada by
Sterling Publishing Co., Inc.1166 Avenue of the Americas,
17th Floor, New York, NY 10036

Everything You Know About Planet Earth is Wrong

Matt Brown

BATSFORD

Contents

Introduction																8

Earth: the basics												**10**
The Earth is only 6,000 years old							12
North is up																		16
The North and South Poles are fixed					18
The world is divided into 24 equal time zones	24
Seas have to wash up against land						30
Australia is the world's largest island				32
Winter is when Earth is furthest from the Sun	34

Unusual territories											**36**

Exploring and mapping the world   **40**

The Earth has been thoroughly mapped   42

We know everything about the Earth's interior   48

Magellan was the first to sail right around the world   50

Until Columbus, people thought the world was flat   54

Everyone now thinks the Earth is round   57

The Earth is a perfect sphere   62

Science of the Earth   **64**

Most volcanoes are in the tropics and have bubbling lava pits   66

The Yellowstone supervolcano is likely to explode soon,

    destroying America   70

We measure earthquakes on the Richter scale   75

Gold is a rare, precious metal   77

The Earth's resources are running out fast   79

Lightning never strikes the same place twice   82

The last ice age ended 12,000 years ago   84

Global warming is a myth   87

Humans have permanently damaged the ozone layer   93

All life on Earth relies on the Sun   95

Boggling geography   **98**

All countries have flags of the same shape   100

Lagos is the capital of Nigeria (and other capital mistakes)   102

Every country has a capital city, home to its government   106

No territory can belong to more than one country   108

Countries of the 'Old World' are much older than
those in the 'New World'   110

Holland and the Netherlands are the same thing   114

Mexico is in South America
(and other mistakes of classification)   116

Florida is the closest US state to Africa (and other
errors in our mental maps)   121

Britain and the UK are the same thing   125

Bits of Earth that never existed   **128**

That's not our name   **133**

River deep, mountain high   **134**

Mount Everest is the world's tallest mountain   136

The Himalayas are the world's longest mountain range   139

The Sahara is the world's biggest desert   141

The Nile is the world's longest river   143

Most of the world's trees are in the Amazon   145

Other myths and misnomers   **147**

Are you pronouncing it wrong?   **152**

Let's start a new wave of false facts   **154**

Index   **156**

Other titles in the series   **158**

About the author   **160**

Introduction

The Earth is a blue ball. Humans have long believed as much, but only in living memory has it been witnessed, recorded and shared. In 1968, the first astronauts to leave the Earth's orbit and swing around the Moon were also the first to see our planet as a sphere. Bill Anders, one of the Apollo 8 crew, later adjudged: 'We came all this way to explore the Moon, and the most important thing is that we discovered the Earth.'

About the same time as the Apollo 8 crew saw Earth from the outside, scientists back home were reworking the inside. A revolutionary theory known as plate tectonics had won newfound acceptance. The mechanisms that shape the land we live on finally made sense and were agreed upon. Meanwhile climate scientists were beginning to piece together the evidence for human-accelerated climate change. Satellite data would eventually show a thinning of the ozone layer. And on it went. The second half of the 20th century brought revelations about the planet at unprecedented pace. Even so, much remains in the 'to-do' pile. Very little is known about the deep Earth – the ball of spinning metal at the core of the planet. How did the continental plates arise in the first place? Can we ever predict earthquakes? Oceanographers have surveyed only a minute fraction of the deep seafloor. Even surveys of the land are incomplete.

All of which makes the earth sciences both fascinating and prone to misconception. Many of the key principles were worked out only in living memory. Big holes remain in our knowledge. 'Facts' we might have learned at school have been superseded as new evidence has emerged. Even the gold-standards of trivia are open to doubt. Can we actually be certain that Mount Everest is the world's tallest mountain? Are you sure you know the name of the world's biggest desert, longest river or largest forest? Is the world even round?

This book collects common errors about the Earth. These include misconceptions about geology and other earth sciences, but also some of the biggest bloopers of geography. These are legion. If you thought Maine was the easternmost state of the USA, or that Florida is the closest to Africa, then read on.

I'm aware that the title of the book is contentious; some would say confrontational. As with other volumes in this series, the aim is not to mock the reader, but to feed a lust for knowledge. Debunking and refuting are powerful tools in this quest. We always remember our mistakes. I just discovered that the capital of Lesotho is Maseru. I did not know this before. I will say it over and over again in an attempt to memorize the fact, but I'm pretty sure I'll fail. Give it a day or two and I'll have no recollection of the name. If, on the other hand, I read that the capital of Nigeria is Abuja, this upsets the applecart. I always thought it was Lagos. That's what I learnt as a teenager, and it *was* the capital until 1991. Somehow Abuja's been running the show for most of my life, and I never noticed. Egg on face. Now, this I will remember.

Each topic in the book begins with a misconception, which is then debunked. Some topics represent widespread misunderstandings ('before Columbus, everyone thought the world was flat'). Others are no longer common beliefs ('the Earth is 6,000 years old') but provoke intriguing discussion. Still others are slightly mischievous. These are included for a sense of fun or a love of nitpicking. I hope you will indulge me.

I began this introduction with Apollo 8. The rest of the book keeps its feet on *terra firma*. While I've included short sections about the Earth's shape and seasons, I've avoided other topics that relate to our planet's place in the cosmos. For that, I'd refer the reader to a previous volume *Everything You Know About Space is Wrong*.

So, grab your compass, GPS and rock hammer, and prepare to get digging. Let the nitpicking begin!

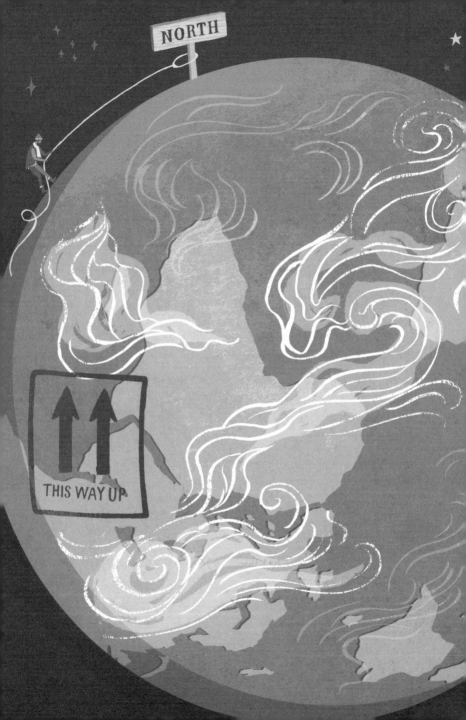

NORTH

THIS WAY UP

Earth: the basics

What is a continent? How old is the Earth?
What's the time, and which way is up? The world
can be a confusing place.

The Earth is only 6,000 years old

The world began on 22 October 4004BCE. At about 6pm. So declared the Most Reverend James Ussher, with a precision that can only be described as flamboyant. The 17th-century Irish archbishop had methodically worked through the 'begat' dates in the Old Testament and woven in other sources to arrive at his figure.

Ussher is mocked today. I'm doing it right now with my flippant tone. His six-millennia figure is the raw side of undercooked, to say the least. The world is almost a million times more hoary than the archbishop would contend. But putting aside (for a paragraph) all the evidence, it should be noted that Ussher did not make the claim lightly. This was no back-of-the-prayer-sheet calculation. The archbishop used cutting-edge astronomical data, including observations from influential German astronomer Johannes Kepler. His biblical dates were cross-referenced with accounts from other ancient sources. He even set the birth of Christ to four years Before Christ, which is self-evidently problematic, but in keeping with historical thought. And, to be fair, Ussher wasn't the only one ploughing this furrow. His English contemporary John Lightfoot had used the same methodology a few years before. Kepler, too, had worked back to a similar date. Even Isaac Newton had a go. He also alighted on a date around 4000BCE. This age for the Earth does not conflict with human records. The earliest surviving buildings, a series of megalithic temples in Malta, are no more than 5,500 years old, while the first written records are from a few hundred years later.

Scientific progress has long since shown, beyond any reasonable – and most unreasonable – doubt, that the world cannot possibly be so young. The first hints came from fossils. What were these alien forms, so unlike any creature alive today, that fell from cliff faces? Ussher and his ilk had an explanation. They were simply the remains of lost creatures, killed by the Biblical flood (a catastrophe that had also shaped the valleys, mountains and hills of the world). The English 17th-century proto-scientist Robert Hooke had a grander view of the ages. The remains of animals recovered from rock, he speculated, '... in all probability will far antedate all the most ancient Monuments of the World ... even [the] very pyramids.' Later scientists began to chip away at the chronology, even as they chiselled into the fossil beds.

One of the key hints to an ancient past comes from rock strata. Many rock faces show distinct bands that vary in shade, colour and rock type. Even before Hooke, sharp-eyed collectors had noticed that different bands were home to different types of fossil. Then came James Hutton. Often called the father of modern geology, this 18th-century Scottish farmer was a sharp observer of nature. He put everything together in his 1788 book *Theory of the Earth*. Hutton believed that the Earth's surface was constantly renewed, driven by subterranean heat. Molten rock was pushed out of the earth, forming new land, hills and mountains. Old rock eroded, and the sediments washed away. These sediments would sink to the seabed where, over time, they would settle into layers (trapping the bodies of animals in the process). With still more time, these might compress into the rock strata we see around us. These in turn would weather, turn to sediment and reform into rock. It was an epic cycle, one that would need aeons of time to revolve. One which continues to turn. In a beautiful phrase, Hutton concluded that the rocks we see today are made from 'materials furnished from the ruins of former continents'. In a less beautiful phrase, someone else called it uniformitarianism.

This was a brilliant insight. Influential, too. Hutton's framework of gradual change over unimaginable spans of time was the metaphorical bedrock of evolutionary theory, developed by Darwin in the next century. Hutton deserves to be a household name alongside the Newtons and Curies of this world. His ideas explained so many features of the natural world, although clinching proof would have to wait for advances in science and technology.

We now know that the Earth is at least 4.5 billion years old. But how? What manner of superhero can pick up a rock and work out its age? The answer is 'a geologist'. The method is ingenious, and not too hard to understand. It is called radiometric dating and was first developed in the early 20th century. If you only retain one thing from this entire book, remember the following chain of reason, because it shows the raw power of a little scientific knowledge.

1. Uranium has a habit of spontaneously changing into lead. Does it all the time. This is radioactive decay, which we all studied at school.

2. This decay happens at a predictable rate, called the half-life. The most common form of uranium (uranium-238) has a half-life of 4.47 billion years. That is, if you left a pure sample of uranium at the back of your drawer for 4.47 billion years, you would find that half had turned to lead.

3. Now, there's a mineral called zircon that turns up in most types of rock. It's very tough and can survive for billions of years under the right conditions. Zircon is made up of zirconium, silicon and oxygen, but it also traps the odd atom of uranium within its crystal. Crucially, when zircons form deep inside the Earth, they *do not* trap lead.

4. Simple conclusion: any lead found in a zircon must come from the decay of uranium.

5. Now all we have to do is measure the relative proportions of uranium and lead in a zircon sample to work out the age of the rock. This is a doddle. It uses a technique called mass spectrometry, which is known to all chemistry undergraduates.

6. We can then use the uranium half-life to work out when the zircon first formed. If the zircon contains much more uranium than lead, then obviously not much has decayed, so this must be a young rock. If it's more like 50/50, then we have a very old sample.

The oldest zircons found so far are about 4.4 billion years old. That means the Earth must be at least this old, and probably a little bit more. A similar figure is found when analyzing rocks from the Moon. The small number of meteorites that came to Earth from Mars also turn out to be of the same extreme vintage. Hence, scientists have concluded that much of the Solar System formed around the same time – about 4.5 billion years ago.

Modern science offers categorical, reproducible evidence that the planet is much, much older than implied by Judeo-Christian tradition. Even so, there are still those who prefer a supernatural rather than a scientific explanation for the creation of the Earth. That's fair enough. Religious worldviews add colour and warmth to our collective accounting of reality. The tale of Noah and the Great Flood is retold even by atheists, in full knowledge that the land was shaped by geological processes. It is a sparkling story, after all. But ideas have half-lives too. Notions of a 6,000-year-old Earth have been decaying for some time, thanks to the ingenuity of geologists.

North is up

To view a map upside down is the fleetest route to confusion. Flip the USA over and you're suddenly confronted with an unfamiliar country that looks like an anteater. At least, it does to me. Spin Australia and you get something that resembles the USA (minus Florida). In 1979, Australian Stuart McArthur published a bestselling world map that truly did reverse the orientation. His home nation is centre-top, with the Soviet Union and Canada 'down under'. Everything is a little bit strange ... and yet equally valid. We only consider north to be 'up' by convention. There are other ways to look at the world.

There is no single reason why north came to be seen as 'up'. The great age of exploration, which saw Europeans pushing into the southern hemisphere for the first time, surely played a role. It was only natural that their cartographers should place home territory in the prime location at the top-centre of the map, with newly discovered realms beneath and to either side. The North Pole also had two navigational attractions. Magnetic compasses point in this direction (though, equally, they also point south), and the prominent Pole Star sits almost directly overhead. A combination of these factors, and other cultural influences, led to our modern, unthinking acceptance that 'North is up'. It's tempting to wonder what might have happened had history turned out differently. Had Earth's greatest explorers set off from the southern hemisphere, would world maps now place Antarctica up top?

The convention towards north is by no means ancient or universal. Many antique maps from the Christian tradition instead put east at the top – the compass direction associated with the rising sun, and the fabled location of the Garden of Eden. The words 'orientation' and 'orient' derive from the act of facing east. The ancient Egyptians also looked to the dawn for the top of the world, or else favoured the south and the source waters of the Nile.

Mapmakers from Islamic territories also had a southward outlook – the direction of the holy city of Mecca from some of the earliest Muslim communities. Placing west at the top of the map is rare. West is where the sun sets and the end of the day is symbolic of death. Even so, North American settlers sometimes drew west at the top of their maps, to indicate the direction of exploration.

Today, almost all world maps are fixed on a projection with a big letter 'N' at the top. The convention is, however, increasingly ignored at the local level. Street-mounted maps of the modern metropolis tend to face in the direction of travel. They swear no fealty to any compass direction. I still regard them with suspicion. Satnavs and handheld devices go still further. They display maps that swing around to show what's ahead, in complete disregard for cardinal points. Some might despair that, as a society, we're losing our grasp of route finding by compass and paper map. I can sympathize. But then, as we've seen, the old way of relating everything to a northern bearing is an artificial construct. GPS devices are a better reflection of reality – not only because they include a 'you are here', and can be updated in real time, but also because they dispense with the artificial notion that north has to be up. That said, I suspect we will always use traditional maps. They still have uses. A paper map won't go blank in a tunnel or flash an error message if a satellite fails. More than this, maps are beautiful objects with the power to bewitch every human I know. Pens, coins, books and paintbrushes belong in the same category.

The North and South Poles are fixed

What happens to a compass at the North Pole? It depends which North Pole we're talking about. The Earth has two locations* that might fulfil the description. The first, and most intuitive is the geographic North Pole. If we imagine that the Earth turns on a giant axle, then the north and south geographic poles are the points at which the axle would emerge from the Earth. Stand stationary on one of these points, and you will turn on the spot, completing a 360-degree rotation every 24 hours.

The geographic North Pole is, by definition, as far north as you can possibly go northwards. But your pocket compass would beg to differ. At the North Pole, its needle points elsewhere, as though there is still more northness to explore. It is aligned with the Earth's magnetic field, not with the Earth's axis. The magnetic North Pole lies hundreds of kilometres from true north.

---

* FOOTNOTE: Just to confuse matters, Earth's magnetic North Pole is technically a magnetic south pole because it attracts the 'north' point of a compass needle. Don't worry about this. It's only by human definition and not an intrinsic quality of the field itself. To add still further complexity, the planet's magnetic field has many fluctuations and local anomalies. It is not symmetrical. One upshot is that the north and south magnetic poles are not antipodes – that is, they cannot be connected by a line drawn through the centre of the Earth.

This much is well-known. What may be less familiar is that the magnetic pole is shifting all the time – not by piddly amounts, but by many kilometres each year. If you could compare a compass reading from the same location both now and 20 years ago, the needle would point in a noticeably different direction – at least from most places on Earth. This has a very real consequence for airports. Every runway is painted with huge digits that represent the number of degrees from magnetic north. These are rounded to the nearest ten and presented as a deca-degree. So, if you see 27 painted on the tarmac, it means the runway points toward 270 degrees, or due west. Over time, as the magnetic pole drifts, the bearing may become increasingly inaccurate. Runway numbers do sometimes need re-assigning and repainting, with all the admin that goes along with it.

At the turn of the 21st century, the magnetic pole was located a little to the west of Ellesmere Island in the extreme north of Canada. It has since migrated hundreds of kilometres north – closer to the geographic pole – and is somewhere beneath the Arctic Ocean. There's little point giving a specific location. In the year between my typing of this sentence and this book's publication, the pole will have moved another 60km (37¼ miles) or so towards Russia. It really does shift.

To see why, we need to understand a little more about the nature of the magnetic poles. The Earth can be considered as a giant magnet. At the heart of the planet is a solid inner core of iron and a liquid outer core of nickel-iron. The liquid metal moves around the core, thanks to both convection currents and the spin of the Earth. Liquid metal in motion generates an electrical current. If you paid attention in physics class, you'll appreciate that moving electric charges (currents) always come with magnetic fields. And that, in a simplified if oversized nutshell, is how the Earth's magnetic field arises.

This spinning core is a complicated, dynamic system. It doesn't hold true and steady but is in constant squirm. The resulting magnetic field is likewise in flux. Its axis rocks back and forth on human timescales, which means the compass reading shifts about over the years.

It gets more extreme. Periodically, and for reasons that remain mysterious, the magnetic field can 'flip'. What we now consider the south magnetic pole will become the north, and vice versa. It has never happened in recorded history, but the evidence is written into the surface of the planet. The iron in lava tends to align with the Earth's magnetic field. As the lava emerges onto the surface or the ocean bed, it cools. The magnetic alignment of its iron is 'frozen' and can be detected by geologists. Rocks from one era show the alignment pointing one way, while those from a later era point the opposite way. The evidence is clear: the Earth's magnetic poles flip often – at least a hundred reversals are imprinted in the rocks. The flip is also quick, at least in geological terms. A complete reversal can happen in just a few hundred years.

Are we due another flip any time soon? It's hard to say*. No pattern has been found in the timings. The last reversal occurred about 780,000 years ago. The one before that was just 200,000 years earlier. Other intervals can last up to 40 million years. When commentators speak of the next flip being 'overdue', we should exercise scepticism. The idea of a fundamental shift in the Earth's behaviour makes for a powerful headline, but the truth is that nobody knows when it might happen.

The reversal of the Earth's magnetic poles sounds pretty ominous. Could it spell doom for civilization as we know it? Probably not. Although the

---

* FOOTNOTE: Unless you're a scaremongering tabloid newspaper editor. 'Earth "under attack from within" and could face "BLACKOUTS for DECADES" as the poles FLIP,' ran one gratuitous headline in January 2018. Such stories are common, unfounded and a leading cause of many misconceptions tackled in this book.

process is swift on geological time scales, it is slow when marked against human lifespans. We would probably see the Earth's magnetic field gradually weaken to a point where it becomes negligible. It would then slowly re-emerge and build up in the reversed orientation. The whole process would take many generations, giving us plenty of time to adapt.

That said, there would be a long to-do list. A reduced or absent magnetic field would remove our protection against radiation from the Sun and outer space. That's bad news all round. Satellites would malfunction, their circuits fried in unshielded orbits. As the field diminishes further, electronics on the surface would become vulnerable. Navigation would be a challenge, without reliable compasses and satellites. Our bodies would also take a pounding. Incidents of cancer would skyrocket, and sunburn could be lethal. Much of this could be mitigated with technology and changing behaviours*, but the diminished magnetic field would have a huge impact on both society and the natural world. The effects could last for many centuries but would eventually improve as the reversed field returned.

The magnetic poles, then, are all over the place. But the geographic North Pole is also a slippery beast to pin down. There is no land at the North Pole, just a thin crust of floating ice. It's so meagre that submarines have surfaced through it. This ice cap grows and shrinks and moves around within the Arctic Ocean. Were you to build a snowman at the North Pole and return a year later, he might still be standing, but not where you left him. (Surely the reason why nobody has yet managed to track down Santa's workshop.) No landmark can be built at the North Pole to mark the location. Not on the surface, at any rate. In 2007, two Russian submersibles successfully planted a titanium flag on the North Pole seabed, 4km (2½ miles) underwater. It was a shrewd, if slightly sinister stunt, intended to bolster Russia's claims to the oil and gas reserves of the Arctic.

---

* FOOTNOTE: Here's another reason to colonize the Moon and Mars. Neither of those bodies has an appreciable magnetic field. The lessons learnt from living in those environments would pay dividends when it comes to surviving on an Earth denuded of its magnetic field.

Even the Russian tricolour is not at the true North Pole. Up top, I defined the geographic pole as the place where an imaginary axle would emerge from the spinning Earth. That was a simplification, for our planet has a slight wobble. Imagine again that giant axle peeping out of the ice. It would not turn on the spot, but would arc around in circles of a few metres, if watched over many years. The geographical North Pole is the average of these positions. The true pole is not fixed to any one spot. There is no permanent 'North Pole', just a moving target.

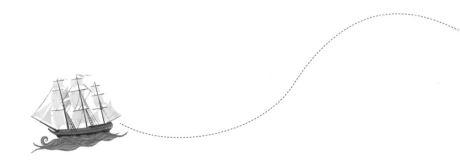

The world is divided into 24 equal time zones

A meridian is an imaginary arc that connects the two poles – half of a great circle. An infinite number of meridians straddle the globe. Move to the right by an inch, or a millimetre, or an angstrom, and you have stepped onto a different meridian. None of these hold any special significance as far as the planet is concerned. But we humans love to impose order. All our meridians are equal, but some are more equal than others.

One imaginary line is held in particular regard. It is known as the Prime Meridian, Zero Meridian, or else the Greenwich Meridian because it was defined from the Greenwich Observatory in London*. The Prime Meridian was set by international agreement (minus the objecting French) in October 1884. Ever since, this has been the worldwide standard for measuring longitude, which is to say how far east or west you are. The meridian passes through the UK, France, Spain, Algeria, Mali, Burkina Faso, Togo, Ghana and Antarctica.

---

* FOOTNOTE: I have to declare an interest and admit a personal fondness for the Prime Meridian. I was born in Cleethorpes, England, a short walk from the meridian's penultimate northern landfall. In 2000, I was living on the Meridian near Greenwich Observatory, right at the centre of space and time during the Millennium celebrations. The fireworks were meek and disappointing, I am sorry to report.

Besides distance, the meridian is also used to mark time. This had long been the case at sea. Greenwich Mean Time was established as early as 1675 to help mariners navigate. The o'clocks of land were a different matter. Until the 1840s, towns and cities measured time by their own sunrise or sunset (or Mean Solar Time, which is slightly different). But dawn might take place at the eastern end of a country many minutes or even hours ahead of sunrise at the western extreme. The USA at this point had something like 300 differing local sun times. This was fine until the world sped up. With the advent of telegraphy and railway timetables, a standardized time was needed to avoid confusion ('is the 10.53 from Tallahassee according to their clock or ours?'). The natural choice was the mariner's friend of Greenwich Mean Time.

By the 1860s, pretty much every clock in England, Scotland and Wales was in line with Greenwich. Other countries would soon look to London for their timekeeping. New Zealand (then a British colony) was first. From 1868, Kiwis set their clocks to 11 hours and 30 minutes ahead of Greenwich. After the 1884 agreement on the Prime Meridian, other countries followed. It took many decades. Only in the 1920s did most of the world agree to be a set number of hours or half hours from London, the system in place today.

Had you not seen a map of time zones before, you might assume it would feature 24 evenly spaced bands, like the stripes on a beach ball, to reflect the 24 hours of the day. Each would be an hour ahead of the previous band, and cover 15 degrees (360 degrees divided by 24). Maps of the world are often divided into these 24 'standard meridians', but political reality makes a mockery of the neat system. A time zone that runs perfectly north–south would seldom respect national boundaries or coastlines. Countries like to keep the same time throughout their territory wherever possible, whether or not one of those 24 meridians happens to pass through. Sometimes, a nation may span multiple time zones (India and China, for example) but, for simplicity's sake, choose to observe just one.

The map of world time zones is fascinating to behold. If you're able, I'd recommend pausing at this paragraph to take a look online. See how many peculiarities you can spot. This is a map of human whims, allegiances and

expedients. The Prime Meridian, for example, passes right through the middle of France. Yet the French do not follow GMT but Central European Time (CET), an hour ahead. France once ran to GMT but changed during Nazi occupation in the Second World War. It never went back. Spain, even further west, is also on CET. Stranger still, the whole of China observes the same local time, even though that girthsome nation spans five standard meridians. In most parts of the world, solar noon – the time when the Sun is highest in the sky – is associated with midday. In western China, it can occur as late as 3pm local time. Another upshot is that you can gain or lose three and a half hours simply by stepping over the border between China and Afghanistan.

Three and a *half* hours? That's right. Not everyone sticks to the tidy +/- 1-hour time-zone regimen. As we've already seen, the very first country to take the lead from Greenwich, New Zealand, did so with a half-hourly division, 11 and a half hours ahead of the colonial master. It's now set to a symmetric 12, but other countries still entertain the oddity. Afghanistan is one of these, set four and a half hours ahead of Greenwich. India (all of it) musters five and a half hours of time difference. Iran, Sri Lanka and Newfoundland are further examples. Nepal, not content with having a unique flag and a mountain that everyone mistakes for the world's tallest (see elsewhere in the book) also has the planet's strangest time zone. It is set five hours and 45 minutes ahead of Greenwich. The Chatham Islands (New Zealand) and Western Australia pull similar tricks. These subdivisions and other peculiarities split the world into 37 different time zones – 13 more than a neat and tidy world of 24 meridians. The number can change. For example, until May 2018 the tally stood at 38. Then, North Korea, which had formerly basked in its own unique time zone, aligned its clocks with South Korea following an easing of tensions. Time will tell if it goes back again.

The situation is further complicated by 'daylight saving time', the practice of teasing clocks forward in the spring or summer to increase the length of the daylit evening. The world is inconsistent here, choosing different dates and durations. Some parts of Australia don't observe daylight saving while others do. In the UK the seasonal clock-twiddling has a most extraordinary effect. For half of the year, people living in Greenwich are not on

Greenwich Mean Time. They are an hour ahead, along with the rest of the UK, on something called British Summer Time. I've lived over 40 years beside the Meridian, and this still hurts my brain.

In fact, Greenwich Mean Time is no longer used for timekeeping. Not officially. Since 1967, the world has regulated its clocks to Coordinated Universal Time (UTC). For everyday informal chit-chat, this is essentially the same as GMT. The two timekeeping systems are never more than 0.9 seconds apart. But if we want to be ultra-precise about time, then UTC is the way to go. It is based on the scientific definition of the second, derived from an atomic clock. GMT is astronomically derived, and has itself been superseded by another astronomical measurement, known as UT1.

Seas have to wash up against land

The terms 'ocean' and 'sea' are used interchangeably by most of us. All that unfathomable wet stuff looks pretty similar. Where does the North Sea end and the Atlantic Ocean begin? Can there really be much difference, or is it all a bit arbitrary? Well, a little bit from column A and a little bit from column B.

At the most basic level, an ocean is big, and a sea is (comparatively) small. The runt of the world's oceans is the Arctic. It covers roughly one and a half times the area of the USA. The largest sea, by contrast, is the Philippine Sea, a little over half the area of the USA. In other words, the smallest ocean takes up three times as much space as the largest sea.

The five oceans are usually defined as the Antarctic or Southern, Arctic, Atlantic, Indian and Pacific. Sometimes, though, the Atlantic and Pacific are subdivided over the equator into north and south moieties, giving a total of seven oceans – or the 'seven seas' if you don't mind a touch of ahistorical confusion. It's important to keep in mind that all of these boundaries are artificial, defined by humans to help make sense of the world. The salt waters of the planet might equally be considered as an interconnected system, a World Ocean.

Seas are found around the edges of oceans, bordered on at least one side by land mass. Some are almost entirely surrounded, as with the Mediterranean and Black Seas. Other times, the borders are hazier, and we must play dot-to-dot with island chains to figure out where sea becomes ocean. But, by and large, seas have coasts. They are waters in which we can paddle.

There is one, and only one, exception to this rule. The Sargasso Sea, over to the western side of the Atlantic, has no land borders. Instead, it is corralled by the North Atlantic Gyre. What sounds for all the world like an obscure R&B sub-genre is, in fact, a hoop of currents that engirdle the Sargasso. The gyre keeps the waters of the Sargasso calm and clear, though they are increasingly besmirched by plastic waste, spun in from without. For that reason, the sea has acquired an even more evocative name, as the North Atlantic Garbage Patch.

Some places we call seas are not considered to be such by hydrologists. Salt lakes such as the Aral Sea, Dead Sea and Caspian Sea are not connected to the World Ocean and have very different ecosystems. The Sea of Galilee, famed from holy texts, is even further from the definition. It is a freshwater lake. Then, of course, there are the powdery seas of other worlds, such as the Sea of Tranquility on the Moon.

Australia is the world's largest island

Australia is massive. At around 7.7 million sq. km (3 million sq. miles), it is the sixth largest country on Earth. France could fit inside 12 times over, if only it would tessellate. You could pack in three Argentinas or a brace of Indias. *Three thousand* Hong Kongs, give or take. It is so large that whole swathes of its interior have never been surveyed from the ground. Most geographers consider it a continental landmass – like Antarctica – rather than a conventional island. On those terms, the world's largest island is usually reckoned as Greenland.

Size isn't the only factor. Australia is by far the greatest landmass on the Australian tectonic plate. By contrast, Greenland plays second fiddle to the combined bulk of Canada, the USA and Mexico on the North American Plate. Australia's biology is also unique. Many of its indigenous animals are found nowhere else on Earth – another continental hallmark. These distinctions combine into a persuasive case for classifying Australia as a continent rather than an island. Ultimately, though, the dividing line is negotiable. It is down to subjective definition.

The flipside of this story comes with its own misconceptions. Greenland is indeed the world's biggest island, but it's not as large as sometimes imagined. Head over to any of the major online maps (or a paper Atlas if you're lucky enough to own such an antique treasure) and take a look at the place. In most depictions, Greenland dwarfs Australia. This is a limitation of map projection. There is no way to depict the globe on a two-dimensional surface without introducing major distortions. The commonest views put the skewed regions at the top and bottom. Hence, northern territories like Greenland are stretched.

Let's return to Antarctica, which I so breezily classified as a continent at the start of this section. It is widely accepted as a continent – albeit one with no permanent population and limited fauna and flora. Its status can be questioned, however. The lands of Antarctica are covered in an ice sheet of confounding thickness – up to 5km (just over 3 miles). If we could somehow remove all that ice, we would find that the underlying land is not one big island but many smaller pieces of land (very small pieces, if we removed the ice by melting and added to global sea level). If Antarctica were in warmer climes, we might not regard it as an independent continent, but as an archipelago belonging to another continent – like the Philippines in Asia. Greenland, too, might not be one single land beneath its thick ice sheets. Disputed evidence suggests that it may, in fact, comprise three distinct land masses. If true, one of them would still, most likely, be the largest in the world as Greenland is roughly three times the size of the next contender, New Guinea.

Winter is when Earth is furthest from the Sun

Sometimes the simplest explanation is not the best. Every child wonders why we have seasons*. What makes the leaves fall off the trees? Why is one half of the year colder than the other? The easy answer, and one believed by many adults, is that the Earth is closer to the Sun in warmer seasons, and further away during the cold months.

This explanation has two golden merits. The simple relationship between proximity to fire and personal warmth is easy to understand. Anyone, even a lethargic dachshund, can grasp it. From there, it's a tiny leap to imagine the Sun as a roaring fire and the Earth dipping in close for the warmer months. Ergo summer and winter. The story also chimes in well with at least one scientific fact. Our planet circles the Sun in an elliptical orbit, which by definition means it strays further out during certain parts of its cycle. We have a ready-made explanation for the seasons that a small child might understand.

This seductively simple story is easily trashed. If winter is caused by the Earth moving away from the Sun, then we'd expect everywhere on the planet to decrease in temperature at the same time. Yet we're all familiar

---

* FOOTNOTE: I'm speaking here with the bias of somebody living in a temperate climate. Those closer to the equator, in the tropics, do not experience such marked changes in season, for reasons that will become clear in the main text.

with the idea of Australians basking in Christmas sunshine, while Canadians hunker down against the snows. When it's winter in the northern hemisphere, it's summer to the south; and vice versa. Likewise, those living on the equator experience little change in temperature throughout the year – although many places have a 'wet season' and a 'dry season'.

It's true that the Earth's distance from the Sun does vary, but not by much. The effect on temperatures is minute. Instead, seasons are all about the tilt of the planet. Imagine a giant stick passing through the Earth from pole to pole – this is the planet's axis, around which it revolves. That rod does not point straight up and down with respect to the planet's orbit. Rather, it is tilted at 23.5 degrees – about the angle you might attempt with a ladder against a wall. This means that different parts of the Earth receive different amounts of energy from the Sun.

For half of the year, the southern hemisphere is directed towards the star, and receives a bigger dose of rays. During the other half of the year, it's the north's turn to lounge in sustained glow, while the south gets less and at a more oblique angle. (If you've ever tried to start a fire with a magnifying glass, you'll know that angled sunlight isn't as warming as more direct rays.) The equator, halfway between the two, receives near-constant radiation at all times of year.

Unusual territories

What is a country? The definition is not as obvious as we might assume. Is Palestine a country? Is Taiwan? In each case, some would say yes, and some would say no. Wales is a country, and a fine country at that. It has its own language, international football team and National Assembly. Yet it does not embuttock a seat at the United Nations, NATO or the World Trade Organization. The United Kingdom acts on its behalf. Israel seems like a solid country, yet 31 members of the UN do not recognize it as such. And what do we make of Antarctica?

Other regions have shifting or poorly defined borders thanks to conflict or political wrangling. Buffer zones and demilitarized zones are to be found throughout the world. There are many such examples. Below are a few of the more curious situations in which the neat conception of well-defined nation states becomes tentative.

Bir Tawil: Part of Africa has slipped down the back of the sofa. The area of Bir Tawil covers some 2,060 sq. km (795 sq. miles) – roughly half a Rhode Island or six Isle of Wights – in the borders between Egypt and Sudan. Nobody wants it. This spurned quadrilateral was conjured into being at the turn of the 20th century, when two rival versions of the border were drawn up. To this day, the neighbouring countries dispute ownership of an adjacent parcel of land, but nobody cares for this barren anomaly, which has no permanent population. This unusual '*terra nullius*' status has attracted numerous chancers – usually westerners – who claim the territory for themselves. In 2014, a Virginian farmer planted a flag in Bir Tawil and proclaimed himself head of state of 'North Sudan'. All this so his six-year-old daughter could style herself as a princess. Reaction ranged from 'Aww, what a dad', to 'Grrr, what a despicable neo-imperialist'. Nobody, save perhaps his daughter, took the claim seriously.

Dahala Khagrabari: The border between India and Bangladesh does not run straight and true. It twists and turns around every fencepost, creating a fractal frontier. The boundary folds in on itself at several locations, creating narrow corridors and numerous enclaves. Until recently, 102 pockets of India were isolated within Bangladesh, with a similar number on the vice versa. How this pebble-dashed border came to be is not entirely certain. One story says the enclaves were created as gambling prizes in the 18th century; another attributes their creation to the random drops of ink from a map-maker's pen. However they first arose, life in the enclaves could be difficult. Many were not formally administered by either nation, and inhabitants were effectively stateless.

Some of the enclaves came with their own counter-enclaves – small areas of Bangladesh, say, within Indian enclaves of Bangladesh. Dahala Khagrabari was the most confusing of all. This 7,000m^2 (1.7-acre) piece of farmland belonged to India, but found itself within a Bangladeshi village, inside an Indian enclave, within wider Bangladesh. It was the only third-order enclave in the world until ceded to Bangladesh in 2015. That year saw the two governments swap over some 162 enclaves – at a stroke deleting most of the world's stock of pocket territories. The planet's craziest border is now a little more rational.

Kaliningrad Oblast: This piece of Russia is geographically cut off from the mother country, surrounded by the European Union (and NATO) states of Poland and Lithuania. The Baltic region was, for much of its history, German in character. Its chief town of Kaliningrad was formerly known as Königsberg, and home to the philosopher Immanuel Kant. It was annexed by the Soviet Union at the end of the Second World War, with the expulsion of most of the German people. It has since remained part of Russia.

Northern Cyprus: The border of this small territory is well defined, yet only recognized by one other country: Turkey. The Turks laid claim to the northern portion of the island of Cyprus in 1974, in response to an attempted annexation by Greece. This quasi-state is separated from the rest of Cyprus (a full European Union member) by a buffer zone, patrolled by a UN peacekeeping force. Remarkably, some 10,000 people live within the buffer zone, which also slices the capital city of Nicosia in two.

The political geography of Cyprus is further complicated by the continued presence of the former colonial power. The British flag still flies over 3 per cent of the island, on areas to the south and north-east known as Akrotiri and Dhekelia. These 'Sovereign Base Areas' are British Overseas Territories, predominantly occupied by the military. They are leftovers from before Cypriot independence in 1960. Just to add further layers of complication, Dhekelia straddles Cyprus, Northern Cyprus and the buffer zone, and contains several Cypriot enclaves.

Puerto Rico: Although the borders of this Caribbean territory are easy to define (it is an island, after all), its political status is less clear-cut. Puerto Rico is tightly within the ambit of the USA but is not one of the 50 states. Puerto Ricans are officially recognized as citizens of the USA and can move freely around that country. However, they do not have a vote in the United States Congress, and cannot take part in US elections.

Somaliland: Where in the world will the next sovereign state emerge? Somaliland is a likely contender. The north-western third of Somalia declared independence back in 1991. It is internationally recognized as an autonomous region of Somalia, but neither the UN nor any country recognizes its statehood. Despite this, Somaliland has made a good stab at running itself like a proper country. It has its own parliament, passports, currency (the Somaliland shilling) and central bank. Further, the would-be state has kept largely out of the chaotic war that has ravaged wider Somalia. It is arguably in better shape than the parent nation. But breaking up is so very hard to do. Putting aside a web of regional complications, the international community is always hesitant to acknowledge breakaway states – it sets a dangerous precedent for other separatist movements.

Vatican City: One of only three states that are true enclaves (the other two are Lesotho and San Marino), Vatican City holds many unique distinctions. It is the smallest state in the world by both population and area. Home to just 1,000 people, it is no bigger than many rural villages. More than half of the territory is gardens – which is both admirable and bonkers. It is not a member of the UN, though the sovereign entity (let's not go there) of the Holy See does have observer status. Vatican City is also one of just two states to have a square flag (the other is Switzerland).

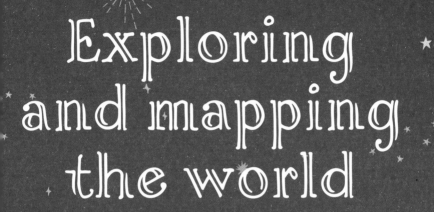

Exploring
and mapping
the world

Bloopers from the Age of Discovery,
and holes in the modern map.

The Earth has been thoroughly mapped

On 14 December 1911, Roald Amundsen planted the Norwegian flag at the South Pole (or thereabouts – his instruments were not precise enough to hit the spot on the nose). The achievement capped almost half a millennium of discovery. It marked the end of the Colombian Age, to borrow the term of English geographer Halford Mackinder. Those *terrae incognitae* that once surrounded the known world had all been filled in. Indeed, the 'known world' as a concept had ceased to exist. Now, it was *all* known. With this last great adventure, the conquest of Antarctica*, human feet had sampled every crook of the planet. The world was charted, complete, comprehended.

So it might have seemed, but the Earth is a big place. Our planet's surface covers some 510 trillion sq. m (roughly 5,500,000,000,000,000 sq. ft, though the conversion is worthless as nobody can imagine these numbers). Walking or swimming at a brisk 2m (6½ft) per second, it would take 255 trillion seconds to pass through every square metre (10¾ sq. ft) on Earth. In other words, and units, you would have to toil without rest for over 194 million years. Still up for the challenge? Not so fast. I've assumed

---

* FOOTNOTE: The question of who first beheld the geographic North Pole is open to debate. Two competing expeditions, led by Frederick Cook (1908) and Robert Edwin Peary (1909), both clambered over the roof of the world, but neither had reliable proof. Roald Amundsen has a better shout. He took an airship over the North Pole in 1926, the first time a visit was properly documented. The first verifiable boot print didn't come until 1948, when three Soviet planes landed nearby on a scientific mission.

a flat surface, which is patently not the case. If you factor in all the hills, mountains, valleys and trenches, then the journey is incalculable. No explorer could ever see it all, or even a significant fraction.

We should also bear in mind that the Earth is ever-changing. Coastlines erode; islands form from undersea volcanoes; every year the ice caps get a little thinner. When I was a child, the Aral Sea in Kazakhstan was counted among the largest lakes in the world. Now it is little more than ponds in a desert. You might complete your 8,000-year jaunt only to find your starting point radically changed.

Fine, you might think, but we don't need to walk and swim the planet. We have drones and satellites, radar and lasers to scope out the details. I can examine the cliffs of Taiwan from my bathtub, using my waterproof smartphone. With a glide and a tap of my index finger, I can plot the quickest route from Chipping Sodbury to Vladivostok*. Surely, by now,

---

* FOOTNOTE: 12,128km (7,536 miles) and a six-day, five-hour drive according to my disturbingly assured maps app.

the whole planet is accurately charted? It is not. Satellites can only image land that their sensors can 'see'. It's a doddle to survey open plains or deserts from space. What's more, satellite imagery has revealed dozens of ruins in remote locations that would have been difficult to spy from the ground. But you run into problems if the land is covered in dense forest, or riddled with deep canyons. Modern satellite technology can reveal a certain amount, but the data are superficial compared to the input of a boots-on-ground survey.

Sometimes, features can dodge the map because nobody's taken the trouble to look. A headline-grabbing example is the forest of Mount Mabu in northern Mozambique. This rainforest, the largest of its type in Africa, was unknown to science until 2005. The site was only 'discovered'* with the advent of online satellite maps. A whole rainforest had gone completely undetected until the 21st century, when it turned up on a computer screen in England. Needless to say, it was quickly dubbed the 'Google forest'. Scientific expeditions have since uncovered many new species, and additional populations of threatened species.

The forests of the world hide many further secrets that have evaded geographers and surveyors. They pop up all the time. In 2007, the lost city of Angamuco was uncovered in western Mexico. The city thrived between 1000 and 1350CE and was built by the Purépecha – rivals of the Aztecs. This was no mean settlement lost among the shrubbery. Recent laser scanning has shown that Angamuco had about 40,000 buildings, as many as Manhattan. Further south, laser scanning is routinely plucking wonders from the Guatemalan jungle. Some 60,000 Mayan structures, part of a vast network of cities, fortifications and farms, have been rediscovered by aerial reconnaissance. The history of Cambodia, meanwhile, is undergoing a major rewrite. Laser mapping has revealed unknown cities in the jungle, which add up to a civilization that may

---

* FOOTNOTE: Those living in the area already knew about this rich forest, obviously. There are, however, no known references to the forest in scientific literature before the 2005 online discovery.

have been the largest in the world 800 years ago. The technology is still new; what will it find in the years ahead?

The Earth conceals other realms, opaque to satellites or drones, and absent from world maps. The only way to chart a cave system is to send in a human. There are millions of subterranean spaces around the globe, carved by natural processes over millions of years. Many are unexplored. Some caves are sealed from the outside world. How many is anybody's guess. Exotic species of life thrive in these hidden environments. Movile Cave in Romania, for example, was first uncovered in 1986. Forty-eight species have been recorded in its lightless, poisonous interior, 33 of which are found nowhere else.

And then there are the oceans. According to a well-known platitude, we know more about the surface of Mars than we do about the ocean bed. This is true, at least topographically. We have better maps of the surface of distant Pluto than we do of much of our home planet. Why? Because of all that water.

At their deepest, the oceans stretch down further than Mount Everest soars. The world's supreme basement is a place called Challenger Deep in the Pacific's Mariana Trench. It is well named. At almost 11,000m (just over 36,000ft) below the surface, this is a challenging depth to reach, even with remote-controlled subs. Here, the waters are pitch black, with pressures a thousand times those at the surface. Only three humans have descended this far (one of whom was the film director James Cameron, in 2012). Four times as many people have walked on the Moon.

Challenger Deep is an extreme, but most of the ocean floor is under depths that demand sophisticated and expensive submersibles. Mapping these regions with human or robotic presence is further hindered by the lack of visibility and intense pressure, which would crush all but the most robust instruments. Surveys must be performed from the surface. The earliest mappers used plumb lines, reeled out from boats to the seabed. The method gives an accurate depth but is laborious, and only provides information about a single point each time. Today, oceanographers use sonar – the sound-bouncing technique beloved of bats. By measuring the time it takes sound waves to return to the surface, researchers can build up a three-dimensional image of the seabed. But the oceans are vast. Huge fleets would be needed to make even a partial map.

At the time of writing, the US National Ocean service estimates that less than 5 per cent of the ocean floor is accurately charted. The rest is covered to a resolution of 5km (just over 3 miles); anything smaller than this size does not show up. Efforts are now underway to change that. The SeaBed 2030 initiative hopes to thrust that figure up to 100 per cent by the end of the 2020s. It will combine existing data with new surveys to build up a comprehensive picture of the ocean floor. The project will no doubt uncover many new wonders of the deep ocean, including the thousands of ships and aircraft that have sunk without trace over the centuries. Accurate maps will also stimulate interest from mining companies, looking for new sources of minerals, oil and metals. Would-be prospectors are currently barred by international law from exploiting the deep oceans, but promising leads would reopen the argument.

Could a whole continent await discovery? Kind of. For obvious reasons, Antarctica is the least explored landmass on Earth. Most human activity is limited to the shores, or tightly defined trekking routes to the South Pole. Very little of the continent has been scanned by human eye, at least not from ground level. Further, 98 per cent of the continent is covered in ice sheet. And it's *one hell* of an ice sheet. The mean depth is 2.2km (1⅓ miles), but it can be twice as thick. Imagine a carpet of frozen water as deep as Manhattan is wide.

An estimated three-fifths of all the fresh water on the planet is locked up in Antarctica's ice sheet. Were it to melt, sea levels would rise enough to require a Brobdingnagian set of waders for the Statue of Liberty. Beneath all that ice is a never-beheld landmass. Its contours have been mapped, crudely, by a barrage of techniques, but we still know precious little about this hidden geology. Lakes, volcanoes, mountains, fossils and even life may be waiting deep below the ice. Who knows what lies beneath?

We know everything about the Earth's interior

Even if we were to map every inch of the planet's surface – including the seafloor and land buried beneath ice sheets; even if we rooted out every cave system in the world, and followed every jungle path; then still, the planet would hide its secrets from us. What goes on in the deeper Earth is still largely mysterious. Astronauts and yacht-dwellers aside, most of us spend our days moving about on the crust of the planet. This rocky layer is only a thin shell – much as the shell of an egg forms but a minute percentage of the ovular substance.

If we could tunnel down just 32km (almost 20 miles) – a moderate walking distance on the surface – we would hit another layer called the mantle. This layer is much thicker, reaching down almost 2,900km (about 1,800 miles). It too is made of rock, but rock that has become molten under intense temperature and pressure. Imagine rock that has the consistency of thick caramel, only with none of the happy mouthfeel.

Deeper still is the core. The Earth's innermost sanctum is a big place. This is a ball the size of Mars. It is as close to me, or you, or anyone, as Hong Kong is from Tokyo. Yet we shall never visit nor photograph this inhospitable sphere. It comes in two layers: an inner core of solid iron, and an outer core of liquid nickel-iron. That inner core is staggeringly, unimaginably hot. Scientists estimate its temperature at 5,430°C (9,806°F), similar to the surface of the Sun.

Much is still mysterious in these inaccessible regions. The deepest hole ever drilled, the Kola Superdeep Borehole, is a mere 12.3km (7⅔ miles). That's only 0.4 per cent of the way to the outermost part of the core, or 0.2 per cent of the distance to the centre of the Earth. We can get a metaphorical taste for the mantle, just 32km down, by examining volcanoes (see page 66). Magma and lava originate in this layer, although they are under very different conditions of temperature and pressure by the time they reach the surface. We can further intuit the nature of the core and mantle by monitoring seismic waves. As these ripple through the planet, they are bent and slowed by denser material, just as light is affected when it hits the water of a swimming pool. Scientists long ago worked out the likely materials at different depths thanks to the characteristic time delay on these waves.

Everything else we know about the core and mantle comes from measuring their effects up above. Convection in the mantle is thought to drive plate tectonics, for example, while the Earth's magnetic field is generated by motions in the molten iron core. Breakthroughs in our understanding of these inner layers will no doubt come in the next 100 years, and we may even drill a borehole down to the mantle. But it seems doubtful we will ever sample the planet's core – that moon-dwarfing ball of iron round which everything we love is built.

Magellan was the first to sail right around the world

Ferdinand Magellan (c.1480–1521) is rightly hailed as one of the great explorers. The Portuguese sailor is a household name all over the planet he was the first to circumnavigate. His name is today celebrated at all levels of cartography – from the Strait of Magellan at the tip of South America to the two dwarf galaxies known as the Magellanic Clouds. But did he really sail right around the world?

Magellan embarked on his epic voyage from Spain in 1519. After many adventures, the round-the-world expedition finally made it home three years later in 1522. The journey took a heavy toll. Of the 270 crew who had set out, only 18 returned alive. Magellan was not among them.

Magellan's mission was to discover a western route to the Spice Islands, now part of Indonesia and known as the Maluku Islands or the Moluccas. European nobility was enchanted by nutmeg, cloves and mace, rare spices that could only be found and cultivated on these islands. Huge wealth awaited anyone who could find an economic way to transport the commodities. The known route round the tip of Africa was lengthy and hazardous. Could a shortcut be found to the west? It was the old dream of Columbus, who had crossed the Atlantic in the hope of reaching the Indies. Magellan, under the patronage of the King of Spain, was to try again, sailing round the Americas and on to Asia. It was the 16th-century equivalent of a Moon Shot – a dangerous, risk-all adventure with the potential to redefine the world.

The expedition set out in September 1519. After crossing the Atlantic and hugging the coast of South America, Magellan discovered a sea route that avoided the southern tip of the continent and would later be known as the Strait of Magellan. In November 1520, more than a year after setting sail, the crew entered the Pacific. Europeans had spied this great body of water before*, but it fell to Magellan to bestow a lasting name on the world's largest ocean. He dubbed it *Mar Pacifico*, after the Spanish and Portuguese word for peaceful. Had he turned up in more squally conditions, world maps might now present the Tempestuous Ocean.

The fleet, now reduced to three vessels after a mutiny and a shipwreck, headed out into this daunting expanse. Its extent was unknown, and greatly underestimated in the conjectural maps of the time. The crew little guessed they had months of sailing before them. Imagine the scenario: at sea for a quarter of a year, with food stocks depleting, no sight of land and little idea of the distance ahead. Finally, in March 1521, they spotted the Marianas and the island of Guam, no doubt to hearty cheers.

It was a prelude to tragedy. A month later, the expedition reached the eastern edge of the Philippines, where the ships were guided by natives to the island of Cebu. Magellan and his crew soon grew friendly with the inhabitants to the point where they agreed to help the Cebu attack their enemies on a neighbouring island. Magellan himself led the charge. He was quickly cornered, shot with a dart, stabbed and beaten to death. His remains were never recovered.

---

* FOOTNOTE: The Spanish explorer Vasco Núñez de Balboa (c.1475–1519) was the first European to gaze out over that ocean. He led an expedition over the isthmus of Panama in 1513, after spotting the ocean from a mountaintop. On reaching the coast, Balboa walked into the water, held his sword aloft and claimed possession of the new sea and all adjoining lands for Spain. If his declaration held any power, then Australia, Canada, Russia, the USA and many others would all be Spanish. Magellan is often cited as the first to reach the Pacific. This is untrue, but he was the first European to do any serious sailing in it.

Far from being the first man to circumnavigate the globe, Magellan had barely made it past the halfway point when he fell in this local turf war. His surviving crew, though, muddled on. The two remaining ships achieved their primary mission of reaching the Spice Islands half a year later. They then crossed the Indian Ocean and rounded the tip of Africa, before sailing back to Spain in September 1522.

The expedition had set out to find a westerly route to the Spice Islands. Box ticked. But the experimental route was both longer and deadlier than sailing east. The single remaining ship limped home with plenty of spice, but after three years of sailing in which almost 93 per cent of the original crew had died or fled. You don't need a doctorate in 16th-century maritime economics to see the problem. This was never going to be a sane way to ship spices back to Europe.

Looking at the wider picture, Magellan's fateful mission was anything but a failure. His crews were the first Europeans to enter the Pacific, sail around South America and discover the island of Guam and the Marianas. They were the first westerners to reach the Philippines. They even discovered a new species of penguin, later named the Magellanic penguin (*Spheniscus magellanicus*) in the leader's honour. More importantly, his expedition had demonstrated that the world could be circumnavigated. An intellectual door was now open. A complete geography of the world lay within reach.

It should be noted that, if his earlier travels are taken into account, then Magellan did indeed traverse the full globe. Our man had previously visited the Spice Islands via the traditional east-sailing route. These lie further east than his place of death on the island of Cebu. Over the course of two trips – one heading east, one heading west – Magellan had sampled every degree of longitude, the first person to do so. His slave, christened as Enrique, may have gone one step further, as the first man to complete a full circuit in one direction. Enrique had joined Magellan on an earlier voyage to Malacca in Malaysia. From here, he sailed west to Portugal with Magellan. He stuck with the explorer during the later round-the-world trip, which again sailed westward. After the death of Magellan, he was left at Cebu to an unknown fate. Some have speculated that he may have returned to his native Malacca. If so, Enrique may have been the first to travel right around the world in one direction.

The first people to circumnavigate the world in one voyage are the 18 crewmen who made it back to Spain after Magellan's death, under the command of Juan Sebastián Elcano. These 18 had not set off to loop the planet; the plan was to find the Spice Islands then head back by the same route. But after the arduous Pacific crossing and the death of their leader, the men chose the simpler route home, and thereby made history. Their valuable cargo carried a small profit, but none of the men were handsomely paid. It would be almost 60 years before the next complete circumnavigation, this time by England's Sir Francis Drake.

Until Columbus, people thought the world was flat

Brave Columbus. When he set off across the Atlantic in 1492, he was heading off the map. Here be dragons* or – worse – a sheer plummet off the edge of the world. All his peers believed the planet was flat. Columbus thought otherwise and was determined to prove them wrong.

It's a myth, of course. The opposite is true. Most of Columbus's contemporaries, and certainly his financial backers, regarded the Earth as a globe. The knowledge stretched back many centuries, even into Greek antiquity. Pythagoras, Aristotle, Euclid and later Ptolemy all assumed a spherical world, though some of their peers did not. By 200BCE another Greek, geographer Eratosthenes, had even calculated the planet's circumference to within about 10 per cent of the true figure. Even scholars writing in the so-called Dark Ages generally preferred a spherical Earth over a flat world. That view survived as the Western orthodoxy into Columbus's

---

* FOOTNOTE: The phrase 'here be dragons' does not appear on any known antique map and is a modern invention. Many maps do, however, include endearing doodles of dragons and other beasts on their margins. Among the more overblown is the beautiful *Carta Marina* by Swedish priest and scholar Olaus Magnus. This 1539 map of the Nordic countries contains dozens of peculiar sea beasts, including a couple that might pass for dragons. It is freely available online.

time. Thus the intrepid sailor of the day held no fear of a bottomless waterfall at the threshold of the seas.

Uneducated people, if they thought about it at all, might well have assumed that the world was flat. Few European scholars had doubts. After all, the evidence was there for anyone to see. During a lunar eclipse the Earth's shadow falls upon the Moon with a pronounced curve. That proves that our world is round, but not necessarily spherical. Proof of the latter can be seen on the high seas. The masts of a tall ship are visible on the horizon before the hull, thanks to the curvature of the Earth. Seek out examples online if you're not in a position to test this for yourself – the effect is rather eerie.

The story of Columbus and the flat Earth is usually attributed to American writer Washington Irving, who wrote a biography in 1828. Irving pitted Columbus against Catholic theologians, who insisted the Earth was flat. No evidence for this exists. Almost all writers in the Middle Ages, most of whom were attached to the church, speak of a round Earth. Coincidentally, the oldest surviving globe of the Earth, known as the *Erdapfel* (meaning 'earth apple'), dates from 1492, the very year of Columbus's first voyage. Word had not yet reached Europe of his discoveries, and the Americas do not feature on the orb.

Columbus himself was a firm believer in a spherical Earth. The whole point of his first voyage was to find a western route to Asia, when previously everyone had voyaged east. He got his maths wrong, though. A misreading of Eratosthenes led him to underestimate the circumference of the Earth. This is why he believed he'd reached Asia when he'd merely crossed the Atlantic to the Americas.

While we're dealing with Columbus, let's address some of the other misconceptions about his voyages. Most famously, the explorer was not the first European to find the Americas. The 11th-century expedition of Norse explorer Leif Erikson reached Newfoundland almost 500 years earlier, and other crews followed in his wake. And, of course, millions of humans already lived in the Americas, the descendants of those who had migrated across a land bridge from Asia, eons before. Columbus's big contribution – or calamity, depending on your view – was to kickstart a wave of colonization. The Americas were treated as a European possession, with concomitant acts of pillage and genocide against the native peoples. This slaughter also raises questions over whether Columbus should, in fact, be hailed as a hero.

While he's chiefly noted for his 1492 voyage to the Americas, Columbus gamely crossed the Atlantic Ocean on eight occasions (four times in each direction). He never set foot in what we now call the United States of America, and only briefly touched land in South America (the first European to do so – not even the Vikings managed this). Columbus spent most of his time in the Bahamas, Hispaniola and various agreeable places along the central American coast. And who can blame him.

Most people, I suspect, would guess that Columbus was Spanish or Portuguese. Though he lived in both these regions, his hometown was Genoa, in what is now Italy. Even the name is wrong. At least, nobody at the time would have called him Christopher Columbus. His Italian name was either Cristoforo Colombo or Christoffa Corombo. The Spanish knew him as Cristóbal Colón. As with so many great figures from history, Columbus straddles the boundary between myth and reality.

Everyone now thinks the Earth is round

On 24 March 2018, one of the more unusual launches in the history of rocketry took place in the Mojave Desert, California, USA. A stubby, steam-powered vehicle climbed into clear blue skies, then parachuted down to a bumpy landing. In the cockpit was 'Mad' Mike Hughes, a noted daredevil with ambitions of political office. His long-term goal is to reach space. He wants to prove that the Earth is not a sphere.

The pilot is one of a growing tribe who believe the world is flat, or discus-shaped. It is difficult to argue with flat-Earthers. 'But what about all the photos from space?' is met with 'Faked'; 'Are all those astronauts lying?' is countered with 'Elaborate hoax'. Most flat-Earthers confine themselves to the comments boxes of the Internet but a few, like Hughes, are determined to prove their case.

Hughes's flight was a dummy run. The tiny vehicle had no hope of reaching space, and barely topped 0.5km (⅓ mile). His crowd-funded ride was more of a PR exercise; a rallying call for the resurgent movement of flat-Earthers. It would have been simpler, cheaper and less risky to launch a high-altitude balloon with a video camera. But Hughes wants to see it for himself. 'Do I believe the Earth is shaped like a Frisbee? I believe it is,' he told the press. 'Do I know for sure? No. That's why I want to go up in space.' He's now working on bigger rockets that might fulfil his ambition.

In a way, Hughes is behaving like a model scientist. The scientific method would have us ignore our prejudices and run objective tests on reality. Few of us question the Earth's shape. We're taught from a young age that it is spherical. We've seen the photos that prove it. We accept a round Earth at face value. But Hughes has doubts. He wants to test for himself. This is in the spirit of science. *Nullius in verba* – 'on the word of no one' – is the motto of the Royal Society, the oldest scientific society in the world. Hughes stubbornly refuses to take the word of *everyone*.

The flat-Earth movement is growing fast, fuelled by the Internet and social media. Online fora concentrate the credulous. Some 50,000 people follow the Flat Earth Society's Twitter account. According to Google Trends, searches for the phrase 'flat Earth' have gone up tenfold since January 2015. In 2018, a YouGov poll found that only 66 per cent of American 18–24-year-olds are confident that the world is a sphere. Sites like YouTube are awash with videos that 'prove' the Earth is a plane, while a sustained campaign of clever memes has found traction on Twitter. (The Flat Earth Society does not claim members 'all over the globe', as one mischievous counter-meme suggested.) Nearly all can be dismissed with the barest scrutiny. Yet the idea of contradicting received wisdom is an attractive one.

These modern flat-Earthers may be deluded, but at least they subscribe to a venerable tradition. As we've seen, notions of a two-dimensional world go

back to the ancients. Despite all evidence to the contrary, the idea has had its champions ever since. An English writer called Samuel Rowbotham (1816–84) was the first to turn the idea into some kind of modern 'movement'. His works of 'Zetetic astronomy' claim to have empirical evidence against a spherical Earth. Rowbotham was influential. After his death, the torch was passed on to a follower named Lady Elizabeth Blount. She founded a periodical with a reassuringly down-to-earth title, the *Earth not a Globe Review*. The movement petered out somewhat during the war years. Then, in 1956, Samuel Shenton set up the International Flat Earth Society.

Note the date. This was one year before the first artificial satellite, Sputnik 1, was put into orbit by the Soviet Union*. From that moment, it became very difficult to sustain a belief in a flat Earth. An artificial celestial ball was circling overhead, and anyone with an amateur radio set could hear it pass by. A decade later, and the Apollo moon missions sent back persuasive imagery of the beautiful blue bauble that could not possibly be flat.

So, who are the modern flat-Earthers, and do they really, genuinely, honestly believe in the pancake planet? As with any belief system, their outlooks are varied. Many are trolls – people who've put little thought into the matter but peddle nonsense to provoke a reaction. Flat-Earthism is yet another cause for anyone who likes picking anti-intellectual fights with 'so-called experts'. Conversely, one might seek a flat Earth as an intellectual challenge. We can agree that the Earth is a sphere, and yet take delight in trying to find ingenious alternatives.

---

* FOOTNOTE: Still earlier launches had photographed the curve of the Earth, an oft-forgotten chapter in the conquest of space. Suborbital rockets from the United States had captured images of the spherical planet as early as 1946. See my earlier book *Everything You Know About Space Is Wrong* for further discussion.

Still others – I should think a minority – hold genuine beliefs. These are also varied. One school of flat-thought has the world on a horizontal plane that stretches outward forever. You can't sail off the end of this Earth because you'll never reach it. An alternative view places our seas and continents on a disc, Terry Pratchett-style. The North Pole is at the centre of the disc, with Antarctica wrapping 360 degrees around the edge.

Whatever the persuasion of a pizza-shaped planet, believers agree that there must be some kind of conspiracy to hide the true nature of the Earth. All the footage from space exploration has to be faked. This is hardly feasible. Photos of a ball-shaped Earth have been sent back from space by numerous players, including countries (USA, Russia, Japan, European nations and China) and private companies (who can forget the SpaceX Tesla?). Are they all in cahoots? If so, why?

According to one theory, NASA and co. have never launched anything into space. As the Flat Earth Society says, 'The Earth is portrayed as round in NASA media because NASA thinks it's round. They are not running a real space program, so they wouldn't know what shape the earth truly takes.' This is self-evidently daft. Rockets have reached orbit, no question. Millions of people have watched launches with their own eyes (myself included). 'Ah, but they only reach a certain height, and then fall back to the sea unobserved,' say the doubters. Well, OK. So how do we explain GPS signals, satellite TV and other services that rely on permanent sentinels in the sky? There is no shortage of tech-savvy people around who could spot if these signals were being spoofed by land-based alternatives. Besides, we can see satellites and the space station passing overhead with the naked eye. Many more are visible with an amateur telescope. I suppose you could fake these with high-altitude planes in constant, predictable circulation, but the cost would be astronomical. If we accept that satellites are travelling high above the Earth, then surely some of them have cameras (or people) who would be able to confirm the planet's flatness or curvature.

There are many other counter-arguments, which I won't retread here. Most readers will recognize flat-Earthism for what it is: silly. Debunking is futile. The Earth's shape can be tested in many ways. If you have even a slight doubt, make enquiries about local projects to launch high-altitude balloons.

You've seen them on the news. They usually carry novelty items, like Lego figures or fried chicken, as part of a PR stunt. Many schools have launched them too, for educational purposes. Such balloons cannot reach space, but they can float high enough to visualize the curvature of the Earth. Of course, a hardened refusenik might say that this footage is faked too, or just an optical illusion, or a warping of the lens at low temperature and pressure. These half-baked explanations are easy to invent, and easy to dismiss. Besides, everyone knows the Earth is really supported on the backs of four elephants who are themselves positioned on the shell of a giant turtle, right?

The Earth is a perfect sphere

Earth may look spherical when viewed in space photos, and most globes are perfect balls. But the true Earth bulges slightly in the middle and is squashed slightly at the poles. Technically, then, it is an oblate spheroid and not a sphere*.

In human terms, the Earth's bulge is pretty big. The diameter between two opposite points on the equator is greater than that from pole to pole by 42.7km (26½ miles). That's about the distance of a marathon. The effect on the circumference is, naturally, even more pronounced. If you're planning a charity walk right around the Earth, you might consider following a meridian (north–south) route, rather than trekking round the equator. A polar circumnavigation is shorter by 139km (86½ miles), though you'd have to pack warmer clothes. These numbers seem considerable, but, compared to the overall size of the Earth they are not (though see page 137 for an unexpected consequence). The 42.7km bulge at the equator compares with a total diameter of 12,756km (7,926 miles) – it is 0.3 per cent of the planet's girth. You'd never notice it.

---

* FOOTNOTE: This is the sole circumstance in which you're likely to encounter the words 'oblate spheroid'. We should change that. It's a nice phrase. Your mission, should you choose to accept it, is to drop the words into everyday conversation, such as 'I would eat the orange, but I have a phobia of oblate spheroids'.

Someone who did was Isaac Newton. The great scientist was the first to suggest the Earth might be an oblate spheroid, long before we had a way of seeing the planet from space. Newton rightly reasoned that a spinning body should always bulge in the middle thanks to centrifugal force. This is not only true of the Earth, but every other planet, moon and object of size within the Solar System (and beyond).

The bulging of the Earth has a curious consequence. If you stand on the equator, you're slightly further from the centre of the planet than if you stand at one of the poles. You are further from the centre of gravity, and therefore (according to classical physics) feel slightly less of a gravitational tug. The upshot is that you'd weigh about 0.5 pet cent less at the equator than at the North Pole (the difference in centrifugal forces between the two regions also plays a part). A foolproof strategy for losing weight, then, is to move closer to the equator.

Science of the Earth

Ozone holes, volcanic cones,
drilling zones and earthly groans.

Most volcanoes are in the tropics and have bubbling lava pits

15 April 2010 was an historic day for my home town of London. The skies above the city – and much of Northern Europe – were free of human taint for the first time since the start of the Industrial Revolution. The belching factories of yore had long gone, and London's famous pea-souper smogs were a thing of the past. But another stain was absent that day, and in the days that followed. Not a single plane or contrail could be seen in the skies. Londoners enjoyed a perfect streak-free blue firmament for the first time in living memory.

The cause was a leviathan cloud of ash. It was almost invisible in the skies over London – at least from the ground – but was nevertheless a threat to aircraft. The tiny particles might have caused engine failure or damaged the metal fuselage. Airports remained closed for several days until the cloud had blown over. Northern Europe had been grounded by a volcano.

The culprit was an Icelandic volcano called Eyjafjallajökull* – bane of tongue-tied newsreaders as well as air travellers. The eruption was neither big nor violent. It just happened to be particularly ash-heavy and occurred

---

* FOOTNOTE: Eyjafjallajökull roughly translates as 'island mountain glacier' and is properly the name of the ice cap rather than the underlying volcano. See page 152 for proper pronunciation.

when the winds were blowing toward continental Europe. The resulting chaos served as a wake-up to Westerners. Contrary to popular imagination, volcanoes are not all found in exotic, tropical locations. They are spread more or less evenly at all latitudes. And, as Eyjafjallajökull showed, volcanoes can have an influence far removed from their physical location.

The idea that volcanos must be tall, conical structures thrusting out of tropical rainforests is largely a Hollywood invention, a bias towards the cinematic grandeur; the monster in paradise. Any movie volcano must also include a bubbling lava pit – handy for dispatching villains.

In the real world, volcanoes come in many shapes and sizes, and can be found in all climates. Most, but not all, are clustered along the boundaries between continental plates. The most celebrated chain is the 'Ring of Fire', a 40,000km (almost 25,000 mile) horseshoe that tracks the shores of the Pacific Ocean. This includes territories as diverse as Alaska, Antarctica, Bolivia and Japan. The last of these possesses about 10 per cent of the world's active volcanoes.

Many volcanoes are undisputedly cone-shaped, just as a child might draw. As lava finds its way out of the volcano vent, it cools and solidifies. Over time, the solid remnant accumulates into walls, forcing further lava to pour over the edge like treacle. Gradually, the cone shape builds up into the classic profile. The stereotypical lava lake within is, though, extremely rare.

Only six volcanoes in the world have semi-permanent pools of lava visible from the volcano rim. The largest is usually at Mount Nyiragongo in the forests of the Democratic Republic of Congo. Not all are in such tropical locations. Erta Ale in Ethiopia has the world's most persistent lava lake, which formed in 1906. Far from a cone in a jungle, this

volcano is in a depression in a desert. Mount Erebus, meanwhile, is a menacing presence on the icy shores of Antarctica.

Cones are not the only shape. A shield volcano, like Erta Ale, has a much lower profile, like a circular shield laid on the ground. These volcanoes form when the lava is more viscous. The molten rock tends to flow further before solidifying, and the result can look more like a large hill than a fairy-tale volcano. The islands of Hawaii offer the largest and most famous examples of shield volcanoes.

Caldera volcanoes, meanwhile, are almost the opposite of the archetypal lava-filled cone. Here, we find a large depression, often filled with water. Calderas (from the Latin for cooking pot or cauldron) are formed after particularly violent eruptions, when rock collapses in on the magma chamber. One of the most famous is the Greek island of Santorini, the remnants of a volcanic explosion 3,600 years ago that may have snuffed out the Minoan civilization.

If some random oddball ever asks you to draw the commonest type of volcano, ask for a blue crayon. Volcanologists estimate that 75–80 per cent of all magma release takes place in the ocean. There may be as many as a million submarine volcanoes around the globe, including what may be the largest. Tamu Massif is a huge geological feature in the deep ocean east of Japan. It covers an area similar to Britain and Ireland and rises some 4,460m (14,633ft) from the seafloor. Whether it constitutes a single volcano has yet to be confirmed.

Not all volcanoes occur on the boundaries between tectonic plates. The volcanic islands of Hawaii, for example, are slap-bang in the middle of the Pacific Plate. How did they form? Geologists refer to such examples as hotspots. These are locations where the underlying mantle is unusually hot; so hot that magma is able to rise through the rock above to reach the surface, independent of plate tectonics. The Yellowstone 'supervolcano' is another example of a volcano caused by hotspot. Which leads us on to ...

The Yellowstone supervolcano is likely to explode soon, destroying America

Writing a book about common errors has its risks. To get my facts wrong can be embarrassing, but not half as bad as messing up the clever-clogs 'I think you'll find' counterfact. Of all the stories in this book, I hope most fervently that I haven't got this one wrong, because if the wildest doomsday predictions for Yellowstone come true, then we're all screwed.

Yellowstone National Park in Wyoming is among the most noted natural wonders on the planet. It is a household name, blessed with beauty, wildlife, half the world's geysers and kleptomaniac cartoon bears. In recent years, it's moved from famous to infamous following a torrent of sensational headlines and documentaries. The park is one giant supervolcano. What we have at Yellowstone is a vast magma chamber 80km (50 miles) long and 20km (12½ miles) wide. By some estimates, the molten rock beneath Yellowstone could fill the Grand Canyon more than 11 times over. It makes the surface a hydrothermal wonderland, but also a ticking time bomb.

The true extent of this magma chamber was only discovered in 2013. Its sheer size, coupled with some timely earth tremors led to an eruption of doomsday headlines. Phrases like 'terrifying', 'destroy us all' and 'cost the lives of billions' were deployed by gleeful news editors. The abomination came with a dread backstory. This volcano has erupted with force many times in the past and must surely be revving for a reprise. We're 'long overdue' another knockout punch, warned the tabloids.

Those stories continue to gush out with the regularity of Old Faithful*. Fear makes for good headlines, which drive pageviews and keep websites going. At the time of writing, a news search for the volcano yields particularly absurd results. Headlines include 'Yellowstone Volcano Eruption: Holy text says volcano WILL blow, MELTING world with fire', 'Yellowstone volcano ERUPTION warning: Hundreds of bison dead as fears of mega blast grow' and, my personal favourite, 'Yellowstone VOLCANO WARNING: "Time traveller" from year 6491 in apocalypse prediction'. All are from the online version of the UK's *Daily Express*.

Let's assume, for a deluded moment, that the 'time traveller' and his editor are correct. What would happen if the supervolcano were indeed to erupt? The initial shockwave would be like nothing witnessed in living memory. The largest estimate – widely quoted, though suspiciously never given a source – is a blast of 875,000 megatons. That's 17,500 times more powerful than the largest nuclear bomb ever tested. Even if the yield were a fraction of this, the effects would be devastating. The initial blast, lava flows and hot gases wouldn't be the worst of it. Yellowstone is sparsely populated and a long way from major cities. Plus, increased activity in the lead-up to an eruption would give some time for evacuation. No, the real catastrophe would come later.

Unimaginable quantities of ash, sulfur and other materials would fill the air above the caldera. This would quickly spread to other parts of the United

---

* FOOTNOTE: Yellowstone's and the world's most famous geyser but not, as often assumed, the largest. The Steamboat Geyser, in the same National Park, can blast water up to 91.4m (300ft) in the air – almost twice the spurt of Old Faithful. Unlike its more renowned neighbour, Steamboat can lie dormant for many years at a time, which may explain why it is less well-known. It erupted three times in the spring of 2018, a rarity that sparked another glut of Armageddon headlines.

States and beyond. Salt Lake City, the nearest major conurbation, would find itself covered in a metre of ash. Chicago, Los Angeles and San Francisco would be ankle-deep. Towns as far away as Mexico and New York would gain only a thin layer, but enough to corrupt water supplies and grind up engines. Millions of homes would become uninhabitable. Crops would fail, and those that could withstand the ash might succumb to acid rain. Refugees would flee the region and then the country. Many would starve.

An event of this magnitude could not stay local for long. The effects are hard to predict and depend on the nature of the explosion. At the very least, the global economy would take an unprecedented clobbering, affecting us all. At worst, persistent ash cover would lower worldwide temperatures causing widespread drought and famine. This would not be Armageddon, and the world would not 'melt with fire', but nor would these be pleasant years to witness.

The Yellowstone caldera is likely to explode at some point. Major eruptions have occurred on at least three previous occasions (with dozens of minor flare-ups). The last great eruption was 640,000 years ago, with other blasts at 1.3 and 2.1 million years ago. You might (and people do) conclude that the supervolcano gets angry every 700,000 years, or so. The next one would be due soon. However, extrapolating a trend from three data points is a fool's errand. We cannot be sure that Yellowstone runs to any kind of clock. Volcanoes are complex and unpredictable beasts, which defy all forecast. Even if we do assume a 700,000-year cycle, the next eruption might be a hundred thousand years in the future and still fit the rough pattern.

Indeed, recent studies of the caldera show that the magma chamber is unlikely to blow any time soon. Rapid changes in ground level in the first decade of the 21st century have now slowed. The US Geological Survey estimates the odds of a super-eruption in any given year are around 1 in 730,000. If Yellowstone does erupt, it's far more likely to result in nothing more exotic than lava flow. The event would be highly disruptive to the national park – and no doubt generate a fresh wave of alarmist headlines – but few consequences would trouble the wider country.

The chances of a catastrophic explosion in our lifetimes is very low, but might the caldera be a national security risk in other ways? In 2017, a sinister story began to circulate online. The North Koreans had supposedly developed a plan to strike the volcano with nuclear weapons. A well-positioned blast could rupture the crust, exposing the magma chamber. The artificially induced super-explosion would be doubly deadly – a doomsday ash cloud laced with radioactivity. With one strike, North Korea could effectively destroy the USA – the ultimate victory of David over Goliath.

The story does not hold much credibility. For one thing, North Korea would struggle along with everyone else through the ensuing 'vulcanuclear' winter. Its largely agrarian society, already malnourished and poverty-stricken, would be decimated by the effects – and that's before the inevitable retaliatory strikes from the USA. For another, it's just not feasible. No nuclear weapon ever developed would be capable of cracking open the crust above the volcano. It'd have to destroy, or significantly weaken a layer of rock some 8km (5 miles) deep. Even then, only the smaller, upper magma chamber would be breached. The volcano's true potential for devastation lies in its deeper realms.

The biggest risks to Yellowstone's four million annual visitors are more mundane – slipping, drowning or exposure to the elements. (In case you're wondering, bear attacks account for only eight fatalities since records began.) That's not to say that the park's unique geothermal environment is entirely safe. Yellowstone's hot springs can top 200ºC (392ºF). To fall in is lethal. At least 22 people have perished in this unimaginably distressing way. Earthquakes, too, are a potential threat – much more likely than a super-eruption. A regional quake in 1959 killed 28 people.

We measure earthquakes on the Richter scale

The Richter scale, as we all learn at school, measures the intensity of an earthquake. Ironically, the scale itself is shaky. Although it is often quoted in the press, the Richter scale is today only used by scientists in one part of the world: Hollywood.

The system was devised in the 1930s by seismologists Charles Richter and Beno Gutenberg (you could argue it should be the Gutenberg-Richter scale, particularly as Gutenberg was Richter's mentor). The pair had a very limited, very local purpose for their scale. They wanted to compare and categorize the energy released by earthquakes in just one area of California using one type of seismograph. The Richter scale works well under those particular conditions but is unsuited to other locations. It is also inaccurate at larger magnitudes.

The moment magnitude scale (MMS) was designed to shake things up. This new system, applicable anywhere in the world, was developed in the 1970s. It is now the standard used by all seismologists. When you read about an earthquake measuring 8 on the Richter scale, the writer is almost certainly quoting the moment magnitude scale. This more universal system suffers from an unmemorable name and little public recognition, so the world carries on referencing the Richter. To be fair, the scales are not wildly different from one another. A magnitude 7 quake (at the top of the Richter scale) spells trouble in either system.

Two other misconceptions about the Richter scale persist. It does not measure the amount of damage caused at the surface, but the amount of energy released. Later interpretations added descriptions such as 'moderate to severe damage', or 'some objects may fall off shelves', or 'certain newspapers may shriek that the world is ending'. These make the scale more tangible but can also mislead. A magnitude 6 earthquake, for example, might be more destructive than a magnitude 7 if it occurs closer to the surface or in a populated centre. Second, it's important to remember that both the Richter and the moment magnitude scales are logarithmic. An increase of magnitude 1 indicates a 10-fold increase in the seismograph reading (it's measured by the amplitude of the seismic waves). This means, for example, that a magnitude 8 quake has ten times the shaking amplitude (and 32 times the energy) of a magnitude 7 quake.

The strongest earthquakes tend to take place around the 'Ring of Fire', a horseshoe of geological activity that follows the edges of the Pacific Ocean. The most powerful ever recorded struck the Chilean town of Valdivia in 1960. Measuring 9.5 on the moment magnitude scale, the quake caused widespread devastation, and sent tsunamis across the Pacific to Hawaii and Japan. The death toll is uncertain but might have been as high as 7,000. The second-largest earthquake in recorded history took place in North America. It didn't affect California, as you might expect, but Alaska. The 1964 event in Prince William Sound registered as 9.2. It killed 139 people and resulted in changes to ground height of over 9m (29½ft) in places. Alaska, in fact, suffers more strong earthquakes than all the other US states put together. The sparse population means that the tremors have less of an effect on the human world than, say, a major slip of the San Andreas fault in California.

Gold is a rare, precious metal

How much gold do you suppose is left in the Earth? Not much. We've been mining the stuff for millennia. Somewhere between 100,000 tonnes and a million tonnes has made the journey between the hypogeal and human worlds. Because of its scarcity, the metal has always been carefully recycled and reused. The jewellery we wear today may have been mined in Roman times, or further back still. New sources are rare, and greedily coveted. The California Gold Rush was well named, as thousands sped to western America in pursuit of wealth. The conquistadors of South America were driven on by tales of great cities of gold. Wherever the precious metal is found, it is quickly exploited. Surely there can't be much left.

Around 3,000 tonnes of gold are currently excavated per annum. That is more than at any point in history. Sooner or later the party has to end. Here's the astounding thing, though. There is enough gold beneath our feet to pave over the entire world. And not with a wispy patina. The golden carapace would be several metres thick. Imagine what a delightful bauble that would make, when viewed from the Moon. Unfortunately, we'll never get our paws on it. Most of the Earth's gold is trapped deep down in the planet's core. It is impossible to reach and tenuously distributed. This is a resource that would need god-like powers to retrieve; and what use would a god have with bling?

Humans can only exploit materials from the Earth's crust. The good news is that even this layer has a bountiful supply of gold. It's easy enough to get a rough estimate. We know how abundant gold is in the crust (0.0031 parts per million by one estimate), and we know how deep we can dig (about 4km/2½ miles). Using the circumference of the Earth, we can work out the volume of crust that can be mined. Multiply by the abundance and, hey presto, we're sitting on more than 100 billion tonnes of gold. Everyone on the planet could get married a million times. Fresh wedding rings would still be in stock.

Here we have a conundrum. Gold is perceived as rare; so rare that people will exploit, steal or kill for its lustre. Gold is classed as a precious metal. Yet as we've seen, there's more beneath our feet than the human mind can boggle. Why doesn't someone dig it all up and make a fortune? The problem is one of economics. Just because something is abundant, it does not mean it is cheap to extract. Earth's gold is widely but thinly distributed. You have gold in your back garden (if you have a back garden), albeit at tenuous concentration. With a panning kit and many hours of sifting, you might find a few milligrams, but nothing like enough to impress your suddenly concerned neighbours, let alone your bank manager.

To mine economically, you need a seam of gold – a place where the metal occurs in abundance. That can happen anywhere on the planet, but then most of the planet's surface is ocean bed, or polar ice sheet, or uncooperative desert. A determined prospector could tackle any of these environments, but the price tag would be higher than the value of gold retrieved. Much better to stick with the handful of profitable mines in easier locations. They satisfy demand for now. By the time the mine's productivity drops, the company exploiting it will have found another location, or developed new technology to get more bang-for-the-buck in the existing location. We won't ever 'run out' of new gold, but we will have to keep innovating and exploring to keep up with demand. That's a statement that might be applied to most of the world's other commodities, as we'll now see ...

The Earth's resources are running out fast

Gold is an unusual material. Existing stocks are scrupulously recycled from generation to generation. It is never thrown away like cheaper metals, nor burnt up like gas and oil. We don't need to mine vast quantities each year to keep civilization going. But the same underlying principles of supply and demand govern the mining of other resources.

Take oil and gas. It's often said that these fuels are close to running out, and that we must switch to renewables as soon as possible. That's a laudable goal. Renewables are better for the environment and attractive for reasons of national security. But the argument that we need to switch because of imminent scarcity is problematic. The phrase 'oil reserves', commonly encountered in news reports, may underlie the confusion. In 2016, BP estimated that the world has oil reserves of 1,707 billion barrels. That's enough oil to meet the planet's needs, assuming current growth in demand, until around 2066. Obviously, we need to wean ourselves off oil well before that happens.

That's not how it works, though. 'Oil reserve' is, aptly, a slippery term. The world's reserves comprise all the oil in known locations, which can be legally, economically and technically extracted. Read that definition again, carefully, and you'll spot four moveable goalposts. Tweak any of them, and you can grow the reserves.

1 *Known locations:* these increase all the time, as oil companies explore.

2 *Legal extraction:* the legality of drilling may change. Nobody can exploit the riches of Antarctica thanks to international treaty, for example. Any right-minded person would hope that protection lasts forever. But the flourish of a pen on a new treaty would open up virgin drill sites, again increasing oil reserves.

3 *Economics:* the cost of extracting oil varies from place to place, for all manner of reasons. It can also change. Drilling in the Antarctic, for example, is not only prohibited by international law, but also would not make sense from an economic perspective. The harsh climate and isolation would make it near-impossible to run a profit while stocks last closer to home. Those economics may change in the future, as the climate warms, or as new technology comes online.

4 *Technology:* oil extraction has got easier in recent decades. New tech means that even more oil can be extracted from a site than previous generations thought possible. Meanwhile, the advent of horizontal drilling and fracking have teased out otherwise inaccessible oil. Who knows what the future holds?

The upshot is that oil reserves, for the time being, are going up not down. Clearly, that can't last forever. We're not sitting on a planet of infinite oil. But the crisis point is decades, perhaps generations away. Many analysts predict that we will switch to a renewables-dominated economy long before that time comes. To paraphrase former Saudi oil minister Sheikh Yamani, the Stone Age did not come to an end because of a lack of stones, and nor will the oil age be ended by a shortage of oil.

Similar arguments apply to almost any resource you care to name: rare-earth metals, copper, diamonds, phosphates ... Earth will never truly run out of any. They may become more expensive or environmentally harmful to mine, which would push up prices and have all kinds of effects on the economy and society at large. We may experience short-lived crises, as one supply of a material runs out before affordable alternatives come online. But no resource ever gets close to true exhaustion.

We should also think about the wider picture when considering the demand for resources. What we take from the earth changes over time. For millennia, everybody in northern Europe was giddy for flint. Its sharpened edge was ideal for chopping wood, or cutting meat, or slicing open an enemy. Then everybody moved on to metals. Flint still has its uses, but the modern world could tick along happily without it. Conversely, none of us cared about rare-earth metals a generation ago. Now almost every person in the developed world carries around samples of neodymium, terbium, dysprosium and a dozen other -iums next to their house keys. These obscure elements can be found in every smartphone on the planet. Demand for a given material can change rapidly. A resource under pressure today might become obsolete in a hundred years.

Digging more stuff out of the ground is not the only solution to dwindling resources. Were mining to become uneconomical, suppliers would switch efforts to recovering and recycling stuff already in circulation. That won't work for oil or gas, of course, but stripping defunct gadgets of their rare-earth metals could prove more cost efficient – and environmentally preferable – than extracting these elements from rocks. And then coming generations may look off-world for their raw materials. The asteroids, in particular, are rich in minerals and relatively easy to target. Without an unexpected leap in technology, we're still decades from a scenario in which off-world mining makes economic sense, but it is a long-term prospect.

Lightning never strikes the same place twice

I doubt this adage is believed by anyone who works in the Empire State Building. The New York landmark receives over 20 strikes per year. A video from 2011, easily found online, shows the tower stricken three times in 15 seconds. For those who believe the myth that lightning can never strikes the same place twice, it is the flashiest rebuttal imaginable. The phrase is meant as a comfort or a confidence booster and implies that a rare and essentially random event is not going to repeat. The airline might have lost your luggage on that last flight, but it cannot happen a second time.

Unfortunately, chance doesn't work like that. You are very unlikely to win the lottery twice. But a previous winner has exactly the same odds as a complete newcomer when it comes to a fresh draw. The two events are independent. In the same way, lightning can hit the same person or object on more than one occasion. It's not impossible, but inevitable. Something like a hundred lightning strikes occur every second. That's 3.6 billion a year. Even if they were randomly distributed, some would perforce (and with force) hit the same spot, given enough time.

But lightning is not entirely random. It has its favourite flashpoints. Some parts of the Earth see far more electrical storms than others. Florida, Rwanda and the Himalayas are particularly cursed. The most striking example, pun intended, is the mouth of the Catatumbo River in Venezuela. Here, atmospheric conditions conspire to cause electrical storms on 260 nights of the year, with thousands of strikes each time.

People, too, can take multiple hits. The name of American park ranger Roy C. Sullivan is rarely printed without the adjective 'unenviable'. He holds the Guinness World Record for surviving the most verifiable strikes, sustained between 1942 and 1977. Sullivan was hit on seven occasions in the line of duty, surviving each with only minor injury. On the final occasion, the prone ranger also had to fend off a belligerent bear. He died under mysterious circumstances in 1983, from a gunshot wound.

The last ice age ended 12,000 years ago

In many ways, the Earth is a warm and pleasant place right now. The vast majority of humans live in temperate or subtropical climates where snow is rare or non-existent. We don't see titanic glaciers creeping down from the Arctic. The world is gradually hotting up thanks to the taint of human industry. Strange to report, then, that we are technically still in an ice age.

Although today's climate is warmer than the frigid conditions we associate with woolly mammoths and hunters in bear skins, significant chunks of ice still cover both poles. This is unusual. Over the long lifetime of our planet, an ice-free world is normal. By 'normal', I mean roughly 85 per cent of Earth's history. We just happen to be living in one of those rare times when a map of the world needs a white paintbrush at the top and bottom.

The extreme latitudes have been frozen for the recorded history of our species. Naturally, then, we think that ice caps are completely normal. They are not. Just four other icy periods have been identified in the entire 4.5 billion-year history of the Earth. These are the ice ages, or periods known as icehouse Earth.

During icehouse conditions, ice sheets at the poles wax and wane over thousands of years. Twenty-thousand years ago, the ice was very much in its 'wax' phase. The so-called Last Glacial Maximum saw all of northern Europe covered in ice. In North America, the glaciers ground down as far as Manhattan. The Alps, Andes and Himalayas were partly concealed. The rest of the planet was cooler and drier than now. With so much water locked up in polar ice, global sea levels were considerably lower, creating land bridges between areas that before and after would be separated by seas. It was a very different world.

The ice has since waned. You've probably noticed. Sea levels rose to their modern levels, and the climate warmed. Approximately 12,000 years ago, the polar ice caps had retreated to a point that would look familiar today. The long ice age, which had lasted around 100,000 years was finally over. Only it wasn't. We're still firmly locked into an icehouse period. The ice has dithered for 2.5 million years, sometimes growing, sometimes shrinking but never entirely disappearing. We live in an 'interglacial', a brief warm period where the ice sheets are relatively small. But while they're present at any size, we are technically still in an ice age.

This ice age may last a long time yet. The most enduring cold spell in the geological record, known as the Huronian glaciation, spanned 300 million years – that's 1,500 times longer than the existence of our species. On the other hand, human-accelerated global warming might tip us out of the cycle and prevent a return of the glaciers for a long time. Maybe; maybe not. Recent research suggests that the next glaciation might have been delayed by up to 50,000 years, thanks to the amount of heat-trapping CO_2 we've released into the atmosphere. Then again, further melting of the ice caps might screw with ocean currents such as the Gulf Stream, potentially tipping us back toward a frozen north.

Global warming is a myth

I have no doubts about the reality of global warming. Nor, I'm assuming, will most readers. Climate change is real, and chiefly caused by the industrial activity of humans. The evidence is clear, and almost universally accepted among scientists. This could have been a short chapter; redundant even. Sadly, large numbers of our fellow citizens beg to differ. To them, humans have had no appreciable effect on the Earth's climate. Theirs is not a fringe backlash. Sceptics include many prominent people from President Trump downwards. On the day I write this paragraph, Trump has appointed a climate sceptic as NASA's Chief Administrator – an agency whose tasks include climate research. Probably not for much longer.

What's behind this scepticism? Climate change is an ongoing, gradual process spanning generations. It's not something you will catch in the act by looking out of the window. Nor can you or I verify it on our own. The world's climate is a complex system. We must put our faith in the findings of scientists who are better equipped to investigate, and in the words of politicians, who must take the scientific advice and legislate. But scientists and politicians are not easy to trust by those who despise authority figures. There are more cynical reasons to deny climate change. The directors and shareholders of polluting industries, for example, will never be among the quickest to call for a reduction in fossil fuels. A small contingent, including a few scientists, simply do not accept the data, or have alternative interpretations. Suffice it to say, virtually all climate scientists now agree that the world is warming, and 97 per cent* of reports attribute the effects to human causes.

The mechanisms driving global warming should be familiar. For two centuries or more, human industry has pumped ever-increasing amounts of 'greenhouse gases' – carbon dioxide, water vapour, methane and nitrous oxide – into the atmosphere. Simply put, these gases trap heat from the Sun, hence the analogy with a greenhouse. It's important to note that humans didn't start the greenhouse effect, which is a common misconception. We need it. Without our blanket of water vapour and carbon dioxide, the Earth would be a much cooler place – like Mars – not temperate enough for life as we know it. Rather, humans have perturbed a system that was already in place. The Earth is hotting up; this is linked to a rise in greenhouse gas levels in the atmosphere; and these come from the burning of fossil fuels, compounded by deforestation and intensive farming.

This much is well-known. It has been taught in high school for decades. But the evidence underpinning climate change, and its human origins, is often neglected or forgotten. It is worth refreshing our memories, because this is important stuff. The evidence comes in many forms and has been re-evaluated many times. Here are some of the key points.

Carbon dioxide levels are rising: There is more carbon dioxide in the atmosphere right now than at any point for hundreds of thousands of years. That's startling. But how can we know? Nobody had any inkling that carbon dioxide existed until the 18th century, and yet we have accurate figures that

---

* FOOTNOTE: This is not a figure lifted from a dodgy opinion poll. It is a measure of scientific findings. A 2013 study gathered together some 12,000 reports on climate change and analyzed the conclusions. Of this huge sample, 97 per cent found evidence consistent with anthropogenic ('man-made') climate change. See J. Cook *et al.* 2013, 'Quantifying the consensus on anthropogenic global warming in the scientific literature': iopscience.iop.org/article/10.1088/1748-9326/8/2/024024/meta

go back to a time long before humans walked the Earth. The information is buried in the high Arctic and Antarctic, far away from human populations.

A hole dug into an ice sheet is a tunnel through time. Each winter, a new layer of snow falls upon the sheet. It compresses the settled snow of previous years. These form a cake of distinct bands. As with the rings of a tree, scientists can work out which bands correspond to which years. To do this, they must first extract ice cores. These are vertical poles of ice, withdrawn from deep beneath the ice sheet using special cutting drills. The cores are suffused with tiny bubbles of air – captured pockets of atmosphere from times long past. Each bubble can be dated from the band it sits within and measured for its gas composition. By this simple (if physically challenging) method, we know with some accuracy how levels of carbon dioxide and other greenhouse gases have fluctuated over the past 600,000 years. We can audit the air that our ancestors breathed.

The data show an undulating climate. I can't reproduce the graph here, but you can get a sense by imagining a cartoon sea serpent. Levels of CO_2 go up and down with some regularity, like the sinusoidal body of the beast. The gas peaks every 100,000 years or so, then swings back down. We've been building to another peak over recent millennia, only this time the swing-back isn't happening. The monster's head is rearing up out of the water, far higher than it has peered before. Where previous peaks have never topped 300 parts per million, we're currently up at 400 parts per million – and rising. The effects of carbon dioxide at trapping radiation are well characterized. There is no question that, all other things being equal, more CO_2 leads to more warming. Unlike the Loch Ness monster, the phenomenon is real.

Sea acidity is on the rise: About a third of that extra carbon dioxide is absorbed by the oceans. That's superficially good, because it reduces the amount of gas that can contribute to the greenhouse effect. From the point of view of the fish, it's not so pleasant. Ocean acidity has increased by about 30 per cent since the start of the Industrial Revolution. As the trend continues, some species may not be able to cope. Acidification also contributes to coral bleaching.

Temperatures are going up: Accurate weather records have been kept all over the world for more than a century. When averaged out, the recorded temperature has gone up 1.1°C (2°F) since the late 19th century. That doesn't sound too dramatic, but most of the change has come in the past 30 years or so. Sixteen of the 17 warmest years on record have occurred in the 21st century. The world is warming, and increasingly so.

The ice sheets are shrinking: Most of us don't spend much time thinking about the ice sheets. They cover areas we rarely visit, like Greenland and Antarctica. But ice sheets hold most of the world's fresh water. Were they to melt, the run-off would swamp the oceans. Sea level would rise markedly all over the planet. The sudden influx of fresh water would play havoc with ocean currents and marine ecosystems.

Photographs from space make it pretty clear that the ice sheets are shrinking year on year. When you look at the numbers, it's even more jaw dropping. Greenland may be losing up to 250 cu. km (60 cu. miles) of ice a year. That's an ice cube with sides of roughly four miles long, every 12 months.

Sea levels are rising: As ice sheets melt, the water runs into the surrounding ocean. The unavoidable consequence is an increase in sea level. This is compounded by 'thermal expansion' when water expands in volume as it warms. Global sea levels are about 20cm (7¾in) higher than a century ago. As with mean temperature rise, the effect is speeding up. Projections are difficult, as many factors could feed into the process, but a conservative outcome could be a 65cm (just over 2ft) rise by the end of the century. That would be enough to jeopardize many low-lying coastal areas around the world, from China to the US.

The world's glaciers are retreating: It's not just the polar ice caps that are shrinking. Mountain glaciers are also losing their stature. Ranges like the Himalayas and Rocky Mountains are getting noticeably thinner on top.

Sea ice is declining: There is no land around the North Pole, but the region is permanently covered in sea ice. Each winter, this spreads out to a maximum, before shrinking back in summer. Records show that the annual maximum isn't quite the max it once was, and it's getting worse. The four most feeble years on record are 2015, 2016, 2017 and 2018. Bad news for polar bears, but also for the rest of us. Removing the sea ice is akin to shattering a big white mirror that reflects the Sun's rays. The seas will instead absorb the heat, exacerbating global warming.

Snow isn't settling: Another symptom of warmer temperatures is less snow. Satellites can measure the change in albedo, or reflectivity, of the Earth's land surface over time. Snow cover has decreased over the past five decades and is melting earlier in the year. As with a drop in sea ice, the diminished snow cover reflects less of the Sun's radiant energy, and the land warms up.

Weather is getting more extreme: Anyone who follows the international weather will probably have a gut feeling that things are speeding up. The words blizzard, hurricane, flooding, drought, wildfire and tropical storm seem to come around with increased frequency. But the plural of anecdote is not data. Is there hard evidence that the world is facing more extreme weather?

A 2017 study by the Energy and Climate Intelligence Unit – a UK-based environmental think tank – makes a convincing case. Its authors scanned the recent scientific literature for research into extreme weather. Of the 59 papers they found, 41 concluded that climate change has increased the risk of some form of extreme weather – either its severity or frequency. All the papers looked at different systems and used different methods, but pooling the results offers a strong consensus: the more the world warms, the greater damage we're seeing from extreme weather.

Those are the main lines of evidence for global warming. Each individually is persuasive. Taken together, the case is clear. Clear, that is, if we choose to trust the science. Most of us cannot personally drill an ice core or take global measurements of ocean acidity, so we must have confidence in the findings of scientists and the acuity of their interpretations. There is an irony to climate change. Our rapid technological progress has led to global warming, but it also helped us to detect the problem. Without the battery of satellites and advanced analytical technology, we would know very little about this major threat to our ways of life.

Humans have permanently damaged the ozone layer

If you've ever taken the trouble to sniff a photocopier – and bravo you – then you'll know the smell of ozone. If you haven't, then I'm not sure how to describe it. Cucumbers in a chlorine jus, perhaps. Not pleasant. Ozone is a simple molecule; a triangle of three oxygen atoms. It is O_3 rather than the O_2 our bodies crave. As anyone who lived through the 1980s and '90s will know, it plays a very important role high in the Earth's atmosphere.

Ozone is very good at absorbing ultraviolet radiation from the Sun. UV rays split the trinity into regular oxygen (O_2) and single atoms. Thus occupied, much less of the radiation reaches the lower atmosphere and surface, where it might play havoc with our cells. Skin cancer is a well-known consequence of too much exposure to UV. Without the ozone layer, instances would rocket, as would cases of sunburn and cataracts.

In 1984, a large hole* in the ozone layer was detected over the South Pole. It coincided with depleted levels around the globe. Research soon found the culprit. Molecules called chlorofluorocarbons (CFCs) had infiltrated the upper atmosphere. Here, they readily reacted with ozone, knocking it out of circulation at a faster rate than it could reform. Less ozone meant less

---

* FOOTNOTE: Technically, it's not a hole but a depression, or significant thinning.

protection from UV rays. The problem grew as the layer shrank. A worldwide crisis in public health seemed inevitable.

CFCs are not abundant in nature. The problem was self-inflicted. For decades, aerosol cans and refrigeration units had been leaching the chemicals into the atmosphere. Our modern lifestyles were screwing up the planet. The crisis coincided with widespread awareness about human-induced climate change, and the two issues were commonly conflated. Global warming and ozone depletion are actually very different phenomena, but they screamed the same reproach: 'Humans: look what you have done to the Earth'. Cue a welcome surge in greater environmental awareness and lobbying, and a less welcome deluge of dewy-eyed 'heal the world' pop songs.

It's easy to despair. But there's another side to this story, and one that gives hope. Once CFCs had been identified as the cause of ozone depletion the world came together to sort the problem out. CFCs and related chemicals were banned in the 1987 Montreal Protocol. Within a decade, ozone levels began to stabilize and then recover. The ozone hole is still around but shrinking. Before the end of the century, we should be close to natural coverage once again.

The damage we caused to the ozone layer is lamentable, but it also serves as a timely and inspiring wake-up call. When humans get together, understand the facts and agree to collaborate, even a planet-wide problem can be reversed. There are lessons to be learned here for other international challenges such as antibiotic resistance, epidemics and, of course, global warming. This message is celebrated by the United Nations every year on 16 September (the anniversary of the Montreal Protocol), as the International Day for the Preservation of the Ozone Layer. Make a note to toast the better side of human ingenuity, with a glass of champagne from your CFC-free refrigerator.

All life on Earth
relies on the Sun

Science can move fast. When I was at school, just a couple of decades ago if I'm being dishonest, we learnt of nine planets in the Solar System. No planets had yet been detected around other stars. We've since lost a local world, thanks to Pluto's reclassification. By the time you read this, the tally of known planets will stand at 4,000.

Such is the pace of change, and not just in the heavens. Another key plank of school science was the idea that all life relies on the Sun. Plants need it to photosynthesize. Animals need to eat those plants, or else swallow other animals that in turn fed on the plants. All of them need the warmth and energy that can only be provided by a ball of plasma more than 100 times the width of the Earth, and millions of times hotter.

We've since found otherwise. Whole ecosystems with no reliance on the Sun have now been discovered. This must surely rank among the most astounding yet little-appreciated insights of recent generations. Were the Sun to blink out tomorrow, then thousands of species would carry on contented and oblivious.

Their home could scarcely be less inviting – from our perspective. These creatures live deep on the ocean bed, where the pressure of miles of overhanging water would crush the puny human frame. This is an abode where geology nurtures life. The rebuff of tectonic plates, gradually moving apart, creates hotspots. These are the warmest waters on the planet. Under huge pressure, emboldened with salt, liquid water can exist at temperatures impossible on the surface. It issues from hydrothermal vents at temperatures above 400°C (752°F). Any life caught within this broiling gush would be extinguished, but surrounding waters are heated to more acceptable levels.

The searing waters have another effect. As they emerge from the deep-sea vent, they come into contact with near-freezing sea water. The sudden clash of temperatures causes a precipitation of minerals such as sulfides, which billow from the floor in inky clouds. With time, these build into towering chimneys up to 60m (almost 200ft) tall. They are known as black smokers.

Black smokers were first discovered in 1979 in the east Pacific. They are unique environments. While the surrounding seafloor is barren of life, the hot vents teem with creatures. Hundreds of species have now been catalogued. They range from simple bacteria through to snails, crabs, eels and even octopuses. All are sustained by the vents. The animals feed on mats of microorganisms known as chemoautotrophic bacteria, which take in all the nutrients and energy they need from the hydrothermal towers. These bacteria are truly independent of the Sun*. They live their lives on the heat and energy from below; from the radiant Earth. The animals that feed on these bacteria may be living in the deepest gutter, but they are still partially reliant on the star. Some supplement their diets with 'marine snow' – particles of organic matter that rain down from above. They also need oxygen, which is ultimately derived from photosynthesis in plant life near the surface. But the bacteria themselves are anaerobic (needing no oxygen) and would not care if the Sun disappeared. Some bacterial species even use the faint light of black smokers to photosynthesize.

The existence of sun-dodging organisms raises questions about the possibilities of life elsewhere in the Universe. If bacteria can thrive in the inky blackness of the seabed, then why not in the oceans of other bodies such as Europa and Enceladus? Some scientists even suggest that life on Earth may have started at hydrothermal vents, then evolved to live in the wider seas. It is a tantalizing thought. We all began as a side effect of geological activity, in a world that never knew the Sun.

---

* FOOTNOTE: A determined pedant might argue that this is not strictly true. Without the Sun, the Earth may not have formed at all. No Sun, means no planet, means no life.

Boggling geography

The seemingly well-ordered world of flags and
borders and cities and states is a right old mess.

All countries have flags of the same shape

Almost all countries have rectangular flags. Nobody is really sure why this conformity exists. There's nothing to stop a show-off state choosing a half moon, or a pentagon, or a piece of cloth shaped like a rampant numbat. But most stick to a plain old rectangle.

That's not to say that all oblong flags are of the same proportion. Eighty-nine of the 195 sovereign states have an aspect ratio of 2:3 – among them China, India and Russia. A further 54 states use a ratio of 1:2. These include Australia, Canada and the UK. The rest opt for a hotchpotch of dimensions including 15:22 (Bolivia), 16:25 (Cambodia), 28:37 (Denmark) and, fussiest of all, 189:335 (El Salvador). The flag of Togo has sides in the Golden Ratio, or $1+\sqrt{5}:2$. The square root of five is an irrational number, and so the flag's width can never be precisely defined by one number. The USA shares its 10:19 flag with Liberia, the Marshall Islands and Micronesia – a good fact to know if you're ever setting a tough pub quiz for vexillologists.

Only three states dispense with an oblong altogether. Vatican City and Switzerland both cherish square flags, a reflection of older military patches. Nepal alone deviates from the quadrilateral. Its flag is formed from a pair of triangles (technically pennons). This is the only national flag that is taller than it is wide. Its basic form dates back hundreds if not thousands of years and yet it is also a work of mathematical sophistication. As outlined in the Nepalese constitution, the flag's precise proportions include reference to 13-figure numbers and four irrational numbers.

Flags with more practical dimensions are often peculiar in other ways. None more so that the flag of the Isle of Man. It sports a trio of legs – a triskelion – which protrude from a bespoke pair of Y-fronts. The flag of Mozambique is the only one to include an AK-47 assault rifle (though Guatemala's has a musket). The flag of Bermuda is the only one to feature a red lion holding up a shipwreck. The wreck in question represents the *Sea Venture*, flagship of the Virginia Company, which was deliberately run aground in 1609 to prevent it sinking in a storm. Until 2011, Libya had the world's simplest flag – nothing more than a plain green rectangle. With the demise of Colonel Gaddafi, an earlier and less remarkable version was reintroduced.

Lagos is the capital of Nigeria (and other capital mistakes)

Capital cities hold a hallowed status in the kingdom of trivia. 'What is the capital city of X?', is a common if lazy question in gameshows, pub quizzes and crosswords. If you're anything like me, you'll be able to list off the capitals of the economically successful, news-making countries, but have a lingering, lifelong sense of guilt at not knowing the chief city of Tajikistan, Malawi or the Solomon Islands*.

Capital cities are such reliable bastions of the quiz question because they are stable, definite facts. In a world of shifting opinions, fake news and alternative truths, it is comforting to have reliable pitons in the cliff face of knowledge. We know that Rome will always be Rome, and all 11 time zones of Russia bend politically to Moscow.

But even capital cities change. Revolution, wars, disasters or the whim of an autocrat President can see the seat of power transfer to an alternative city. It happens more often than you might think, and even in economically developed countries. Take Bonn. The city was the capital of West Germany until 1990, when it lost its status to Berlin in a reunified Germany.

---

* FOOTNOTE: For the record, and to address my own ignorance, these are Dushanbe, Lilongwe and Honiara, respectively.

Nigeria presents another example. Many of us would habitually reply 'Lagos' if asked to name the capital. Yet Lagos has not held that title since 1991. In that year, the Nigerian government decided to shift out of the more populous Lagos to the new city of Abuja. The move put the capital in the centre of the country, in a location more neutral to the many ethnic groups who make up the Nigerian population.

Myanmar followed suit. Not only did that country change its official name from Burma (in 1989, although it took a while to catch on internationally), it also shifted its capital city. Until 2005, the political centre was Rangoon (or Yangon ... it too has changed name). Now it is Naypyidaw. You may never have heard of Naypyidaw. Nobody had until 2006. The brand-new capital was built from scratch on a greenfield site. The reasons behind the move have never been revealed. This is a capital city changed by stealth.

Building a capital from scratch is not a new wheeze. Ancient cities such as Baghdad, Kyoto and Constantinople (now Istanbul) nailed that one in the first millennium. St Petersburg, Russia and Washington DC were laid out in the 18th century. Canberra, Australia was created in the early 20th century. Pakistan developed the city of Islamabad in the early 1960s. Rio de Janeiro had served as the capital of Brazil for almost 200 years* when, in 1960, the seat of power was transferred to the more central location of Brasília. This unique city was built from scratch, steeped in the modernist architecture of Oscar Niemeyer. Rather wonderfully, the original streets form the shape of a giant aeroplane when viewed from above. The city grew from a barren plain to a hub of 2.5 million people in just 50 years.

---

* FOOTNOTE: Less well known is that Rio once served as the capital of Portugal. In 1808, the Portuguese royal family needed a bolt-hole to escape the advances of Napoleon. They chose the colony of Brazil, which was subsequently elevated to the level of kingdom, on an equal footing with the colonizing country. In 1815, Rio was declared the capital of the United Kingdom of Portugal, Brazil and the Algarves, which it remained until 1822. In a unique scenario, the population of Portugal had to look overseas for their kingdom's capital.

Kazakhstan is another country to build entirely new corridors of power. In 1997, the seat of authority wandered 1,207km (750 miles) from the southern city of Almaty to the more central Astana. Like Brasília and Naypyidaw, this too was custom-built, though not from scratch. The area was settled in 1830 as Akmoly, and heavily developed in the Soviet era. Following its assumption of capital status, the newly named city of Astana was extensively remodelled into a cityscape of futuristic buildings. Redevelopment work continues to this day.

For those who like to keep track of such things, here is a list of every shift of official capital city since 1980. These are only the simple cases, and do not include situations where a country has dissolved (e.g. former Yugoslavia) or unified (e.g. Germany).

Sri Lanka: Colombo ➜ Sri Jayawardenepura Kotte (1982)
Ivory Coast: Abidjan ➜ Yamoussoukro (1983)
Micronesia: Kolonia ➜ Palikir (1989)
Nigeria: Lagos ➜ Abuja (1991)
Tanzania: Dar es Salaam ➜ Dodoma (1996)
Kazakhstan: Almaty ➜ Astana (1997)
Myanmar: Yangon (Rangoon) ➜ Naypyidaw (2005)
Palau: Koror City ➜ Ngerulmud (2006)
Equatorial Guinea: Malabo ➜ Oyala (estimated 2020)

That's nine changes in 40 years. Throw in capital cities from countries
that didn't exist in 1980, like Eritrea, South Sudan and the bounty of states
reborn from the former Soviet Union and Yugoslavia, and the world map
I studied in my youth looks very different today.

The political shuffle shows no signs of settling down. Nothing could say
'set in stone' more firmly than the Egyptian capital of Cairo. Indeed, this
ancient habitation on the Nile is adjacent to the most famous set stones in
the world, those of the pyramids of Giza. Now change is in the air. In 2015,
the Egyptian government placed a question mark over the future of Cairo as
its capital city. Its streets are among the most crowded on the planet, and
the desire for a blank slate is understandable. The government has teased an
as-yet-unnamed development 45km (28 miles) south-west of Cairo, with
space for 5–7 million people. Among the promised modern wonders are
a park twice the size of New York's Central Park, a towering monument
resembling the Eiffel Tower and a major theme park akin to four
Disney Worlds. Uniquely, the city's construction would be financed by
private-sector companies, including Chinese investment, and not by the
Egyptian state. It is a bold experiment in urban planning that, at the time
of writing, remains on the drawing board. Indonesia and the new state
of South Sudan are also exploring the idea of new capitals.

Every country has a capital city, home to its government

Having given a few examples of their impermanence, let's take a step back and try to define what a capital city actually represents. It is trickier than one might expect.

I've lived, for half my life, in London. It has all the trappings one might expect from a capital city. It is the seat of government and the main residence of the head of state. The judiciary is based here. It is by far the largest city in the UK, geographically, economically and by population. No rational person could possibly dispute that it is a capital city. Yet it's not so clear-cut. London has never been declared the capital of England or the UK. It has no formal charter or constitutional keepsake to enshrine this status. The city is not even called 'London' in most formal arenas. Its administrative units include Greater London, Inner London, Outer London, the City of London, the City of Westminster, and many other divisions, but rarely just 'London'*. We call London the capital city by tradition only, not by any legislative or constitutional decree. The same is true of Paris.

If one can have doubts over such cast-iron capitals as London and Paris, then what muddied waters might we find elsewhere in the world? The

---

* FOOTNOTE: See *Everything You Know About London is Wrong* for more discussion on this nugget.

idealized capital city of the imagination might bring together all the machinery of state in one place, along with economic clout and a large population. In the real world, many capital cities do not encapsulate all of these things.

Several states keep their official capital separate from the seat of government. The Netherlands offers the most well-known example. Amsterdam is deemed the capital city, not only by quickfire TV quiz shows, but also by the Dutch constitution. Yet the state's muscles are flexed an hour's drive away in The Hague. Here you'll find the legislative and executive branches of government as well as the Supreme Court, major international courts, and most foreign embassies. Similar though not identical set-ups can be found in Benin, Chile, Bolivia, Ivory Coast, Georgia and the Philippines.

Some states have no capital city. That fact seems remarkable on first blush, but let your mind play over it for a few seconds, and you'll see why. The world still contains a handful of city states such as Monaco, Singapore and the Vatican. Each is too tiny to harbour stand-alone cities, and so the concept of a capital is meaningless. The island of Nauru in the Central Pacific is an independent state, despite being less than half the size of Manhattan with a population of just 11,000. It has no official capital, though the town of Yaren is the seat of its parliament.

No territory can belong to more than one country

In our neat and simplistic view of the world, any piece of land or stretch of water must belong to one country, and one country only. There may be disputes or wars over who does in fact own that territory, and some areas are declared 'neutral zones' or 'buffer zones' or 'international waters' – all outside the control of any one state. But is there a third option, a compromise? Are there ever occasions when part of the planet is shared equally between two or more states?

The answer is 'yes'. Lake Constance at the northern foot of the Alps is one example. The borders of Germany, Austria and Switzerland meet beneath its waters. But look at online maps and you'll find little agreement on where. At the time of writing Bing and iOS maps show the three countries meeting at a single point, though in different locations. Google Maps avoids offence by terminating the border lines at the water's edge. The truth is, nobody has ever laid down the boundaries in a formal treaty.

That means there are rival interpretations. Switzerland favours set borders of its own definition, while Germany's position is unclear.

Austria's stance is the most thrilling. It holds that the waters of Lake Constance are equally shared, all the way across, by the three bordering nations. If you were to take a boat out into the lake, you would simultaneously be in Germany, Austria and Switzerland – which is a handy tip if you want to break a most-countries-in-one-holiday personal best. Such a situation, when countries share an area of land or water, is rare, and known as a condominium.

Antarctica might be considered the world's biggest condominium. This spacious realm is jointly controlled by the 53 signatories of the Antarctic Treaty System. Theoretically, no nation can claim sovereignty over any part of the continent. That hasn't stopped Argentina, Australia, Britain, Chile, France, New Zealand and Norway from having a go, though their territories are not universally recognized.

At the other end of the hectarage scale is Pheasant Island. This uninhabited island on the Bidasoa river is rarely visited by humans. It is no more than 200m (656ft) long and contains little but trees, shrubs and ducks (perhaps even a pheasant or two). Its one feature of note is a stone monolith marking a peace treaty, which offers a clue to the island's unique status. Thanks to the terms of the Treaty of the Pyrenees (1659), Pheasant Island flip-flops between France and Spain every six months. On 1 February, the Île des Faisans becomes the Isla de los Faisanes. It is then peacefully handed back on 1 August. This is a temporal border; the one place in the world where you can shift between countries without moving a muscle.

Countries of the 'Old World' are much older than those in the 'New World'

Brits often adopt a jokey air of superiority when talking about the USA. It's a common wisecrack to refer to the States as 'our former colony'. Yet much of the so-called New World is older than the Old World, at least politically.

Dating a country is not as clear-cut as you might assume. By one measure, the USA was born on 4 July 1776, when the original 13 states declared independence from Britain. Or we might take 1781 as the foundation, the year in which Britain formally recognized American independence. Still more persuasive would be the signing of the constitution, which took place in 1787. One might even argue that the current United States of America came into being on 21 August 1959, when Hawaii joined the club as the 50th state (even then, we're ignoring later shifts in borders and a bit of give-and-take with overseas territories).

Back over in the 'Old World' and we find different textures of fuzziness when it comes to statehood. The United Kingdom, for example, was founded in 1707. England, Wales and Scotland (all of medieval origin) were merged together into the same sovereign state. Yet they'd already shared the same ruler since King James VI of Scotland had assumed the throne of England in 1603. The borders of the sovereign state have changed several times since 1707. The most recent overhaul came in 1922 with the partition of Ireland. That year might also be considered the birth of the UK as we know it or, to give it the full title, the United Kingdom of Great Britain and Northern Ireland.

The lesson from this is that it's very difficult to compare like with like when considering the relative ages of countries. By what is arguably the most sensible comparison – the first adoption of the state's modern name – we could say that the UK (formed 1707) is 80 years older than the USA (constitution of 1787). In this case, the New World country really is the newer, but that's not always the case.

The seemingly ancient countries of Europe, for example, are anything but. Italy stands out here. The territories we today associate with that nation were united into the Kingdom of Italy in 1861, though it took a few more years to get everyone onboard. Before that, these lands were shared by oft-feuding entities such as the Grand Duchy of Tuscany and the Kingdom of the Two Sicilies (in case you're wondering, the 'other' Sicily was the lower boot of Italy, centred on Naples). The modern constitution, declaring a Republic of Italy, was not enacted until 1948.

Germany, too, has a turbulent history of shifting borders. For much of its past, the area comprised a confusing jigsaw of city states, personal territories and miniature kingdoms. As late as 1866, the German Confederation included over 40 members. The German Empire came into being in 1871, uniting most of this hotchpotch. Its territories, borders and political direction have mutated many times since. The borders as we know them today were formed only after the Second World War, as the two states known informally as East and West Germany. Modern Germany arrived with Reunification in 1990.

The Middle East offers striking examples. Most people will know that the state of Israel was created in relatively recent times (1948). Many of the other countries of the Middle East are of similar vintage. The region was the cradle of civilization, where cities such as Babylon, Ur and Nineveh sprang up thousands of years ago. The oldest continually inhabited cities in the world – Damascus, Jericho and Aleppo – are all of this region. Yet the current borders of the Middle East were almost entirely drawn up in the

20th century. Pull up a map from before that time and we don't see many familiar names. Much of the territory was part of the Ottoman Empire. It was carved up by the victorious powers in the years following the First World War. Out of this exercise, eventually, came the states of Syria, Iraq, Jordan, Saudi Arabia and others – largely artificial constructs of western diplomats. Their simplistic, straight-line borders are still with us today. They are not the sole cause of the region's troubles, but certainly a factor.

By contrast to the recent states of the Old World, some of the countries of the New World are positively wizened. As we've seen, the USA declared its independence in 1776, but many other countries followed: Haití (1804), Mexico (1810), Venezuela and Paraguay (1811), Argentina (1816), Chile (1818), Costa Rica and Peru (1821), Brazil and Ecuador (1822), and Bolivia and Uruguay (1825). In addition, several countries of Central America jointly declared independence from Spain in 1821 to form the Federal Republic of Central America. Almost the whole of the Americas had settled down into independent states while the likes of Italy and Germany were still in a hundred pieces.

Of course, I'm cherry-picking here. Some countries of the 'old world' have remained intact for centuries, with only minor changes to borders. France has existed in some form since the 9th century, for example. Meanwhile, many nations of the New World only gained independence in the second half of the 20th century. Saint Kitts and Nevis is the newest. It has functioned as a sovereign state since 1983, when it finally broke free of UK rule (though the British monarch still reigns). The point is that handy labels like 'New World' and 'Old World' shouldn't blinker. The terms make sense when applied to the Age of Discovery from a European perspective, or as handy pigeonholes for wines, but say little about modern governance and territory.

Holland and the Netherlands are the same thing

Holland is world famous for its windmills, clogs and tulips, as well as for sticking two fingers up at the sea. Some of these stereotypes are dated, but not nearly so much as calling Holland a country.

We should, of course, speak of the Netherlands when talking about the modern state. Holland is but one small region on the western coast of that country. Actually, it's two: North Holland and South Holland. These regions contain the most famous Dutch cities – including Amsterdam, Rotterdam and The Hague – but the wider Netherlands occupies seven times the area of the Hollands.

There was once a country called Holland. In the early 19th century, these lands served as a client state to Napoleonic France. The Netherlands became the Kingdom of Holland in 1806 under Napoleon's brother Louis (or Lodewijk, as he soon styled himself, in an effort to exude Dutchness). The Kingdom of Holland lasted just four years. Napoleon grew tired of his younger brother's rule and, in 1810, annexed the territory into France. The country was once again known as the Netherlands after the emperor's downfall in 1813.

No country called Holland exists now. The name hasn't troubled atlases for over 200 years. Even so, Holland is a common shorthand for the Netherlands – particularly when referring to the football team. That much is reasonably well known. Less well aired is the fact that the Netherlands is just one of four countries within the wider Kingdom of the Netherlands, headed by the Dutch Royal Family. To find the other three, you have to cross the Atlantic to the Caribbean. The islands of Aruba, Curaçao and Sint Maarten* are also fully-fledged members of the Kingdom of the Netherlands, sunny relics from the days of empire.

It gets still more convoluted. The country (as opposed to the Kingdom) of the Netherlands also includes the Caribbean islands of Sint Eustatius, Bonaire and Saba. Again, these are flag-waving, Dutch-voting, Heineken-swigging parts of the Netherlands, which just happen to be in the Caribbean. Their inhabitants are counted as citizens of the European Union, although the islands are not viewed as member states. They certainly do not consider themselves as living in Holland.

The distinction between Holland, the Netherlands and the Kingdom of the Netherlands is already tangled enough, but what about the Dutch? Where does *that* name come from, and why don't we say 'Netherlanders'? Indeed, inhabitants of that country do refer to themselves as Nederlanders, an ancient term that means 'the people who live low by the sea'. It is a bit of a mouthful, so outsiders favour 'the Dutch'. This word is also ancient, derived from the original Germanic tribe who settled the area. We get Deutsch (of the German people or language) from the same place. Thanks to centuries of Anglo-Dutch rivalry in war and trade, the English language has picked up numerous phrases that refer disparagingly to the Dutch. To have Dutch courage is to be emboldened by alcohol, while double Dutch is an incomprehensible use of language. Less common now are Dutch gold (fake coinage), Dutch bargain (a transaction made while drunk), and Dutch comfort (a situation that isn't great, but could have been worse).

---

* FOOTNOTE: Actually, Sint Maarten is the southern half of the island of St Martin. The northern half, also called Saint Martin, is an overseas territory of France. It is the smallest inhabited island divided between two countries. The French half trades in euros, while the Dutch moiety uses the Netherlands Antillean guilder, but the US dollar is almost universally accepted. I visited on my honeymoon. It is a charming, but confusing place.

Mexico is in South America (and other mistakes of classification)

Where does South America end and North America begin? There is no debate. The answer is apparent from the map. North America is topped by Canada and the USA, then becomes increasingly narrow as we head south through Mexico and Central America. It almost peters out to nothing in the isthmus of Panama. Then, suddenly, the land opens up again as we reach Colombia. This seems as clear-cut a place to put a continental boundary as any on Earth – and certainly much neater than the frontier of Europe and Asia. The very shape of the land makes you want to draw a line south of Panama and say 'this is the border'. All major international organizations agree on this definition.

The boundary between north and south has deeper routes. The continent of South America sits entirely on one tectonic plate, the predictably named South American Plate. Canada, the USA and Mexico also share one patch of crust, the North American Plate. Furthermore, the whole of North America (including Mexico and central America) lies north of the equator, while 90 per cent of South America is below the equator. The case couldn't be clearer. Mexico belongs to North America.

Even so, the country is often grouped mistakenly with the south. The reasons are tied in with historical and cultural circumstance. Canada

and the USA have a chiefly (though of course not exclusively) English colonial background, and still speak that tongue. Mexico has an Iberian colonial background. The predominant language, ethnicity and religion of Mexico are closer to those of South America than anything to the north. But for political, geological and 'just look at the map' reasons, Mexico *is* part of the north – as are the seven countries of Central America to the south, along with the Caribbean.

Speaking of which, what counts as the Caribbean? The term is often applied to any island east of the Gulf of Mexico. To a close approximation, that's not bad. But it's not quite right either. We need to define the extent of the Caribbean Sea carefully. This is bordered to the west by Central America and the south by South America. The northern and eastern boundaries are demarcated by the chain of islands that begins with Cuba and heads east through Haiti, Dominican Republic, Puerto Rico and the claw of small islands that curve down to Venezuela. Spend a few minutes looking at the map, and it all seems rather clear. Islands outside of this ring are not within the Caribbean. These include the Bahamas and the Turks and Caicos islands. These are geographically part of the Atlantic Ocean but are nevertheless strongly grouped with the Caribbean both culturally and politically. Far-off Bermuda is more than 1,600km (1,000 miles) from the Caribbean, but its shared history gives it close ties. Cuba is a bona fide Caribbean island, though its size and cultural similarities to the Hispanic countries of Central and South America often place it in a different mental pigeonhole. A geologist might tell you that Cuba is firmly a North American country – unlike most Caribbean islands, it rests on the North American tectonic plate.

Misconceptions like these pop up all over the globe. Let's try northern Europe. Ask anyone to name the countries of Scandinavia and – unless they come from Scandinavia – chances are they'll get it wrong. The answer might include Denmark, Norway, Sweden, Finland, the Faroes, Iceland and possibly Greenland. In fact, fewer than half of these make the cut. Scandinavia is a grouping of three kingdoms: Denmark, Norway and Sweden. The peoples of these three countries are descended from Germanic tribes. They share similar languages and culture. Consequently, these countries have self-identified as an informal union known as Scandinavia.

Finland is often thrown into the Scandi mix. It's not hard to see why. It shares a similar climate and location on the map and was for many centuries part of Sweden. However, the Finns are ethnically distinct from Scandinavians and speak an unrelated language. Iceland is closer to Scandinavia in language and culture, yet much further away geographically. It does not consider itself Scandinavian. Ditto the Faroe Islands, which are halfway between Scotland and Iceland. This North Sea archipelago is an autonomous country but not a sovereign state. It is part of the Kingdom of Denmark, which also includes Greenland. While only Sweden, Denmark and Norway are considered Scandinavian, all of the territories mentioned above may be conveniently grouped as Nordic countries.

Spin around to the other side of the globe and we find more continental confusion. What is the difference between Australasia and Oceania? It's common for outsiders to mix up the two, or use them interchangeably. Oceania is the name of the continent. It includes Australia, Melanesia (New Guinea and nearby islands), Micronesia (the islands north of Melanesia) and Polynesia (the islands of the central and southern Pacific including New Zealand). Australasia is a much narrower term and more loosely defined. It's commonly used as a shorthand for Australia and New Zealand together, reflecting the close ties of those English-speaking countries. New Guinea and surrounding islands are sometimes included, especially when the term is used geographically.

By contrast, the range of countries collectively known as the 'Middle East' are consistently defined. This trans-continental region includes the countries of the eastern Mediterranean, bookended by Egypt and Turkey; the Arabian Peninsula with Saudi Arabia and the other Gulf States; plus Iraq and Iran. The definition seldom strays further into Africa, Asia or Europe. Few would ever include Pakistan, Sudan or even Afghanistan within the Middle East, even though all have close ties to the area and predominantly Muslim populations.

The term has consensus but is also contentious. What is the Middle East in the middle of? Where is it east of? It is surely no surprise to find that the phrase is of western European origin, and specifically British. More surprising is its recency. Until the early 20th century, the Middle East was more commonly known as the Near East. China, Japan and what we now call South-East Asia were the Far East. Everything in between – including Mesopotamia, the 'stans' of central Asia, and parts of India – was colloquially the Middle East. The modern definition only gained traction during the campaigns of the Second World War. Its first official use by the USA did not come until 1957. The term is now widespread and is even used within the Middle East. Yet in an increasingly globalized world, it feels like an unhelpful label if taken literally.

Florida is the closest
US state to Africa
(and other errors in
our mental maps)

Close your eyes and imagine the shape of Great Britain. Now position, in your mind's eye, the Scottish and Welsh capitals. If you're anything like me, you'll picture Edinburgh over to the extreme east, while Cardiff is getting on for the far west. Besides a decent drive north, you'd have to head east quite a long way to get from Cardiff to Edinburgh. Only, you don't. Take a look at any map with lines of longitude. The two cities are almost exactly aligned. If anything, the Scottish city is slightly further west, with Cardiff centred at 3.18°W and Edinburgh at 3.2°W. Let me say that again: Edinburgh is west of Cardiff. What's going on?

We all carry prejudices and misconceptions about the world's geography. These are borne of pigeonholed thinking, personal ignorance and cultural bias. The Edinburgh anomaly feels weird to those of us who picture the British landmass as running north-south. In reality, this tilted isle is on a 20-degree slant, allowing Edinburgh to peer directly down onto Cardiff. If you're unfamiliar with Britain's geography, then you naturally won't identify with this example. But equivalents can be found all over the world.

We're not helped by our maps. As we've seen in previous sections, projecting a three-dimensional globe onto a flat surface is fraught with complications. It is impossible to do so without introducing distortions. The world maps we're familiar with are not a true depiction of the continental arrangements. The polar regions are usually astonishingly warped. Look for Svalbard on any Mercator-style projection: the Arctic archipelago typically appears to be the same size as India. In fact, it covers an area more than 50 times smaller. As we head to the extreme north or south, lines of longitude fail to converge as they would on a globe. The terrain is tumescent; the Pole apparently infinite.

Mapping and mental shortcomings combine to mislead. What would you say is the closest US state to Africa? My guess would have been Florida. In my head, the sunshine state seems to jut out towards Africa, and its

southerly location puts it on par with the latitudes of that continent. If we look at a world map, the answer seems less certain. The US coast appears to run parallel with the north-west coast of Africa, and any point might be closest. Consider the world as a globe, however, and we get a startling result. Florida is nowhere near the closest point to Africa. A place called Quoddy Head in Maine (specifically its lighthouse) wins that title. It is 5,076km (3,154 miles) from Morocco. By contrast, the closest connection between Florida and Africa is 6,574km (4,085 miles). The curvature of the Earth and a bias for considering coastlines as running north–south fool us (or at least me) into favouring Florida, when in fact another state is almost 1,500km (over 900 miles) closer.

Further examples are easy to find. Prague, in the Czech Republic, feels decidedly like it's in eastern Europe. There's a cultural bias here. The country was part of the Eastern Bloc allied with the USSR during the Cold War, and so it is still considered eastern by many. Yet geographically, it is in the western half of Europe. Prague itself lies further west than territories we'd casually describe as 'Western Europe'. Much of Norway and Sweden, half of Austria, and the southern parts of Italy are all to the east of this 'East European' city.

Europe itself extends further east than may be imagined. The extreme is Cape Flissingsky, a frigid spit of land in the Russian Arctic. It can be found 69°E of the Prime Meridian. This seldom-visited part of Europe is more easterly than anywhere in Iran. With the right snow gear, you can stand in Europe and be further east than Karachi. If you cherry-pick your map pins, then (part of) India lies west of (part of) Europe.

What other counterintuitive cartography can we find? Well, it depends on where you live, who you are, and what prejudices you harbour, but most people, I think, would find some of the following list surprising.

• Alaska is the *easternmost* state in the USA (as well as the furthest north and west). The long chain of the Aleutian Islands, which stretch down from Alaska into the Pacific, run so far west that they cross the International Date Line and end up with easterly latitude.

- On a similar note, it's possible to see Russia from the USA (and vice versa). The islands of Big Diomede and Little Diomede in the Bering Strait are just 3.5km (just over 2 miles) apart. The former is part of Russia, the latter America. While the bigger island is uninhabited, Little Diomede is home to a small permanent population of US citizens, who gaze out over Russia every day.
- Africa is around three times larger than the USA.
- About two-thirds of Africa is north of the equator.
- Meanwhile, nine-tenths of South America is below the equator.
- The southern tip of Africa is a long way from Antarctica – roughly 4,000km (almost 2,500 miles). This is a similar distance to the shortest route from the USA to Europe.
- Chicago in the north of the USA is at the same degree of latitude as Istanbul in southern Europe.
- London is further north than any town in the contiguous USA – by 483km (300 miles).
- Brazil is larger than Australia. Both are wider than the Moon's diameter.
- All of Florida is further south than the Mexico-US land border.

Britain and the UK are the same thing

The countries of the world sparkle with ambiguity. We all say 'America' to mean the United States of America, even though the USA is just one part of the wider Americas. The country of The Netherlands and the territory of Holland are often used interchangeably (see page 114). But nowhere on Earth, absolutely nowhere, causes as much confusion as that group of islands to the north-west of France. I'm talking, of course, about Great Britain. Or the United Kingdom. Or the British Isles. Or England. Or … well, let's try and disentangle the differences.

England: England is a country but not a sovereign state. It gave up that status in 1707, when it chummed up with its neighbours to form the United Kingdom (which is a sovereign state). The two place names are often confused by outsiders, but also by the egocentric English who sometimes see themselves as the most important part of – and effectively synonymous with – the wider UK. England is the most populous country of the United Kingdom, and also contains the capital city, London.

Great Britain: This is the trickiest one. Great Britain can be a geographic term, but it can also be a political term, and it's easy to fall between the cracks. When used in its purest, geographical sense, Great Britain relates to the main island in the region, which includes England, Scotland and Wales. In this usage, Great Britain does not include places like the Isle of Wight or the Orkneys, which are separate islands. Somewhat surprisingly, Great Britain is the world's third most populous island, behind Java in Indonesia and Honshu in Japan.

That said, the term is more often used with a degree of political flavour. It is commonly understood to mean the main island plus all associated islands – basically the UK minus Northern Ireland. Neither Great Britain, nor the United Kingdom include the Isle of Man – a self-governing, dependent territory located between the island of Great Britain and Ireland.

Britain: A confusing shorthand for both the UK and Great Britain. It is without official meaning but is used in the same way that the United States of America is often shortened to just 'America'.

The United Kingdom: Often abbreviated to the UK, this territory's full name is the United Kingdom of Great Britain and Northern Ireland. That title makes it clear that this is a political entity more than a geographical term. The UK is the sovereign state that comprises Great Britain (England, Scotland and Wales), plus Northern Ireland, the north-eastern chunk of the neighbouring island. The four countries have been in alliance since 1921, following the partition of Ireland. Formerly, the whole island of Ireland was part of the UK. Confusingly, people who live in the UK are known as British. That's fine if you live in England, Scotland or Wales, but a little puzzling if you live in Northern Ireland, which is in the UK, but not in Great Britain.

Blighty: Affectionate name that Brits sometimes use to describe their home country. Although it can refer to the UK in general, the word has a distinctly English nuance. The term became widespread in the First World War. It still holds connotations of pluck, resolve and bulldog spirit, elements of the nation's wartime character.

The British Isles: Another geographical term, the British Isles is the collective name for the many islands clustered together north-west of France. These include Great Britain, Ireland, the Isle of Man, the Isles of Scilly, the Shetlands, Orkneys, Hebrides, Channel Islands and thousands of smaller islands. This would seem like one of the easiest definitions to understand. There are no ifs or buts or peculiar boundaries, and all politics is ignored in favour of solid earth. The British Isles is simply all of the bits of land lying in the sea to the north-west of Europe (although the position of the Channel Islands complicates this slightly). Even so, the term is fraught with difficulties. Many in Ireland regard the adjective 'British' as oppressive. Having won freedom from political union with the UK, the Irish understandably have a grievance over the term 'the British Isles'. Even when the name is used with purely geographical intent, it still smacks of overlordship – imagine if the USA were referred to as the British Americas.

The North Atlantic Archipelago: One of several suggested alternatives to the politically awkward phrase 'the British Isles'. It is neutral and inoffensive. It is also wordy and dull. Plus, few people – beyond the compilers of sub-chapters like this one – have ever heard of the term. Other suggestions include the Anglo-Celtic Isles (very Tolkien), 'these isles' (confusing without further context), the Atlantic Archipelago (meh), the Islands of the North Atlantic (what, including the Faroe Islands and Iceland?), and the workaday British-Irish Isles. Britain and Ireland seems to be the best compromise.

The bewildering complexity of these islands does not stop there. What of Ireland, the Republic of Ireland, Northern Ireland, Eire, Ulster, the Channel Islands, the Isle of Man, Jersey, Gibraltar, British Overseas Territories and the Crown dependencies? I think I'm going to have to start a whole new book. Watch this space …

Bits of Earth that never existed

When explorers and cartographers got it wrong:

Atlantis: Surely the most famous mythical land, Atlantis was a great civilization swallowed by the sea. The imaginary island, sometimes a whole continent, first crops up in the writings of Plato around 360BCE. Plato placed Atlantis 'beyond the Pillars of Hercules', which is to say somewhere in the Atlantic Ocean. It seems that he conjured up Atlantis as an allegorical plaything, an imaginary island with which to compare historical cities like Athens. Yet the story of a hubristic society swamped by the waves had lasting appeal, to say the least. Since Renaissance times, Atlantis has been seen by many as an historical fact – a city or kingdom, hidden somewhere beneath the waters west of Europe. Speculation about its precise location remains rife. A cursory search of news sites reveals that Atlantis was recently 'found' at least four times in just a year and a half: close to Mexico in June 2016, near Gibraltar in January 2017, beneath Antarctica in May 2017 and in a Turkish lake in November 2017. It's not even a new craze. 'German Discovers Atlantis in Africa', ran a headline in 1911, putting the vanished island off Togo. 'Fabled Atlantis Found' ran the papers a year later, working up theories that Atlantis was beneath the Azores – an idea posthumously published by another German, the discoverer of Troy Heinrich Schliemann. 'Staggering new claims' of April 2018 have returned Atlantis to the Azores, where strange perpendicular lines have been spied on the seabed using Google Earth. The elusive island has been exposed more times than the identity of Jack the Ripper.

El Dorado: The mythical city of El Dorado started out as a mythical man. It was said that the chief of the Muisca people of present-day Colombia would be ritually covered in gold dust before bathing in a lake. Over time, the tale grew to become a whole city replete with gold and jewels. El Dorado would appear on maps, as though it were a real place just waiting to be reached by a trek through the rainforest. Indeed, many expeditions set out to find the fabled city, including two in the late 16th and early 17th centuries led by the British adventurer Sir Walter Raleigh. No gilded city was ever found, but such expeditions did greatly increase knowledge of the South American continent. El Dorado's name is still invoked as an unobtainable paradise.

Island of California: California got its name two decades before it was discovered. A Spanish romance story of 1510, which translates as 'The Adventures of Esplandián', includes a fictional island called California populated only by black women. When Spanish explorers first reached the thin strip of Baja California in 1533, they believed it to be an island and named it California in tribute to the story. By the end of that decade, further exploration had established the land as a peninsula rather than an island. California is accurately drawn in subsequent charts, including the standard-setting 1569 Mercator world map. All was right with the world, or at least this corner. Then something strange happened. Through a murky combination of misinformation, wilful distortion and cartographic cack-handedness, California became an island again. It first budded off the coast in 1622 in an influential map by Michiel Colijn of Amsterdam. The mistake was plagiarized into orthodoxy. For the rest of the century, and part of the next, California was universally accepted as an island. It would not be until the 1770s – around the time of the founding of the United States of America on the other side of the continent – that Baja California was definitively shown to be a peninsula, not an island.

Lemuria: By the mid-19th century, most of the world's coastlines were charted. Sailing around the world was now routine, and no more continents could possibly await discovery. Or could they?

This was a golden age of natural history. Darwin's theories of evolution had given a new framework to nature. Research expeditions scoured the globe for undocumented species. They noticed something peculiar. Related animals were often found on distant land masses, with no apparent means of migration between the two. A case in point was the lemur. Though indigenous only to Madagascar, lemur-like fossils had been found hundreds of miles away in India. How did they get there? The simplest explanation was that Madagascar and India had once been connected by land, which had since been submerged. The drowned landmass was dubbed Lemuria – the land of the lemurs.

Lemuria became a magnet for mystical belief. Like a nouveau-Atlantis, the missing land was the setting for legends and unlikely origin stories. Some declared it the birthplace of humanity. Perhaps it extended into the Pacific, to hook up with Australia and Easter Island. In the 1880s, the mystic Helena Blavatsky dreamed up a detailed back-story for Lemuria. It had been populated, she reckoned, by hermaphroditic giants, who laid eggs and enjoyed congress with animals. Later fantasists drew maps.

We now know that Madagascar and India were indeed once joined to the same landmass, many millions of years ago. Their separation came about by plate tectonics (they moved apart), rather than sudden inundation. Even so, the lost land of Lemuria lives on in numerous films, songs and video games.

Mountains of Kong and Moon: Pick up a 19th-century map of Africa and you might well see a range of mountains running right across the continent like a belt. The western stretch, running out of Guinea, was known as the Mountains of Kong. The eastern continuation was known as the Mountains of the Moon, legendary source of the Nile. Both ranges are entirely fictional. The Mountains of the Moon date back to antiquity, and are mentioned by Ptolemy in the 2nd century CE. The spurious peaks of Kong first appeared on a map of 1798, which showed the explorations of Mungo Park. Its maker, James Rennell, made up the mountain range to fit his own theories about the course of the Niger River. The creative cartography was subsequently taken as gospel by generations of map-makers. The ranges remained a common feature of African maps until very late in the 19th century, even though nobody had ever glimpsed them.

Sandy Island: In these days of laser measurements and eyes in the sky, we might assume that the world is surveyed in microcosm, but big surprises still happen. Take Sandy Island. This strip of land the size of Manhattan has decorated charts of the Coral Sea since the 19th century. It even appeared on Google Maps as a mysterious black streak between Australia and New Caledonia. Not any more. A survey team visited in 2012, only to find that the island does not exist. It hadn't simply succumbed to rising tides. The ocean was almost 1.6km (1 mile) deep at this point. Sandy Island wasn't there, or anywhere. It never has been. Cartographers now think the island was added to the charts in error. Perhaps the original 19th-century map-maker had seen a floating island of pumice. Maybe a biological feature was mistaken for land. Whatever its origins, the fake island was copied onto later maps and survived into the age of digital mapping.

Thule: The island of Thule is namechecked by a who's-who of classical authors. Pytheas, Strabo, Virgil, Pliny the Elder, Tacitus and others speak of a frozen land to the north of Britain. Some writers even claim to have visited Thule and met the inhabitants. The island appears on numerous maps from the medieval period onward. Yet tracking it down has proved a Thule's errand. Some have suggested that Thule was really Iceland, Greenland or Ireland. Thule could be an Orkney, a Shetland, or a fragment of Norway. Or this may be an island of the imagination, never truly glimpsed; a movable metaphor for the unknown lands of the north.

A genuine Thule does grace the modern atlas, however. One of the Sandwich Islands in the South Atlantic was given the name in the 18th century, in homage to the mythical land. A trading post of Thule was established in western Greenland in 1910. It has since readopted its local name of Qaanaaq, which itself holds the near-mythical status as a palindromic word beginning with Q.

That's not our name

We automatically assume that the names of countries are clear-cut. France is France, and China is China. But the labels we use are often shortened versions of official names. Some countries use entirely different names for themselves than those they present at the Olympics or United Nations. The following partial list gives the common international name for a country, followed by its official international name, and then the local name. Note that variations are possible for some of these, especially if translated from countries who do not use the Latin alphabet.

Albania: Republic of Albania; Shqipëri
Armenia: Republic of Armenia; Hayastan
Austria: Republic of Austria; Österreich
China: People's Republic of China; Zhōnghuá
Croatia: Republic of Croatia; Hrvatska
Egypt: Arab Republic of Egypt; Miṣr
Fiji: Republic of Fiji; Viti
Finland: Republic of Finland; Suomi
Georgia: Georgia; Sakartvelo
Germany: Federal Republic of Germany; Deutschland
Greece: Hellenic Republic; Hellas
Hungary: Hungary; Magyarország
India: Republic of India; Bhārat Gaṇarājya
Ireland: Republic of Ireland; Éire
Japan: Japan; Nippon
Poland: Republic of Poland; Polska
South Korea: Republic of Korea; Hanguk
Sweden: Kingdom of Sweden; Sverige

River deep, mountain high

The tallest, longest and largest
aren't always where you'd expect.

Mount Everest is the world's tallest mountain

The world's most famous mountain is slippery and treacherous – not only for those who seek to climb it, but also for writers. Everest might be a monumental edifice, but rock-solid facts are hard to come by.

Its height is contentious. The official figure has shifted around for various reasons. Do you measure to the snow line or rock line? Who's doing the measuring (politics can play a part), and how (technology certainly plays a part)? The height above sea level currently stands at 8,848m (29,029ft). This figure is not perpetual. The plate movements responsible for creating the Himalayas have not gone away. The range continues to push upwards by a few millimetres every year. Then again, it may also have shrunk. When a devastating earthquake struck Nepal in 2015, it altered land heights across the region. Kathmandu rose up by about 1m (3¼ft). Satellite measurement suggested that Mount Everest may have lost about 2.5cm (1in) in height as a consequence, but follow-up surveys must confirm this.

Even its name is knavish. Mount Everest remembers Sir George Everest (1790–1866), the British Surveyor General of India. The honour was proposed by his successor. Everest disliked the idea. He believed that such a prominent peak should take a local name, and that 'the native of India' would find 'Everest' hard to pronounce. Nevertheless, the name caught on and was cemented in 1865 when the Royal Geographical Society made things official. Everest was right about the pronunciation, though. He insisted that his personal name be pronounced Eve-rest, but everybody since has gone for Ever-est. Then, of course, the name of Everest is only a western, colonial imposition. The mountain had several local names among the Nepalese, Tibetan and Chinese long before the British arrived. There have been numerous calls to re-anoint Everest as Chomolungma or Qomolangma, much as Ayers Rock in Australia is now commonly known as Uluru. The Nepalese name of Sagarmatha is also a contender.

After which lengthy preamble, we have finally reached base camp for this topic. That Everest (or Chomolungma or Sagarmatha) is the tallest mountain in the world would seem an unassailable fact. After all, it's more than 200m (656ft) taller than its nearest rival of K2. Yet again, it depends how you measure.

Everest's height of 8,848m refers to the distance between its summit and sea level. But some mountains carry on below sea level. The most impressive is Mauna Kea, a volcano on the main island of Hawaii. From the sea bed to its summit, Mauna Kea would top 10,200m (almost 33,500ft). If the oceans were drained, then Mauna Kea would, by all measures, be the tallest peak on Earth.

We might demote Everest by further devious means. If we were to measure the distance from the centre of the Earth to the tip of the summit, then Everest would be pipped by Chimborazo in Ecuador. It stands 'just' 6,263m (20,548ft) above sea level but, because the planet bulges close to the equator (see page 62), its peak is further from the *centre of the Earth* than Everest's by some 2,000m (a shade over 6,500ft). The Peruvian mountain of Huascarán would also top Everest for the same reason.

A final candidate might be the Alaskan peak of Denali, formerly known as Mount McKinley. It rises 6,190m (20,308ft) above sea level, seemingly trivial compared with Everest. However, Denali's base-to-peak height is actually bigger than Everest, as the latter mountain rests on top of the Tibetan Plateau, which gives its base a hefty leg up.

In conclusion, Everest is dubiously named, of uncertain height, and only the tallest mountain by the arbitrary standard of height above sea level.

Strangely, given their size, mountains are often mistaken and mixed up. Ask a friend to name the tallest mountain in Europe, for example. Chances are you'll be told Mont Blanc, or the Matterhorn. The former is the tallest in the Alps, at 4,808m (15,774ft). The latter is merely the sixth tallest at 4,478m (14,692ft), but carries fame because of its distinctive, pyramidal profile. Much taller than either is Mount Elbrus in Russia. This stands an impressive 5,642m (18,511ft) – over 1km (⅔ mile) taller than anything else. The prominence is often excluded because it is east of the Black Sea in the Caucasus Mountain – a region that is often regarded as part of Asia rather than Europe. Most authorities, however, include the range within the European continent.

The Himalayas are the world's longest mountain range

Fourteen places on Earth offer views above 8,000m (26,247ft). Ten of them are in the Himalayas. This range of mountains at India's northern borders is truly monumental. Here is Everest. There is K2. Here is Gangkhar Puensum, probably the tallest unclimbed mountain in the world. Himalaya means 'abode of snow' in Sanskrit, and the name is apt. These mountains contain the third largest stockpile of snow and ice on the planet, after the Arctic and Antarctic.

The range stretches some 2,400km (nearly 1,500 miles) across Asia. This mighty pleat formed when the Indian subcontinent, once an island, smashed into the Eurasian tectonic plate. Much of this elevated land was once deep under water. Over millions of years, the collision of plates thrust the limestone seabed into the air. Mountains were formed of spellbinding proportion. Marine fossils are found near their summits, a key piece of evidence for plate tectonics.

As geological features go, the Himalayas are hot off the press. Their vertical surge began 40–50 million years ago. For 99 per cent of its history, Earth had no Himalayas. The piton-clawed dinosaurs never contemplated an ascent – with the exception of the birds, their line died out 25 million years before the range could out-loom a molehill. Indeed, moles and their hills are themselves older than these adolescent peaks. Like any teenager, the Himalayas are still growing, and with it comes growing pains. The Indian plate continues to drive into the Eurasian plate in what is known as a 'thrust fault'. The movement is small, about 5cm (2in) a year, but it's enough to cause earthquakes in the region. Grab a satellite view of the planet, and the full prominence of the range becomes clear. You can almost feel the squeeze and thrust of this plate boundary.

Because of their monumentality and iconic status, the Himalayas might be assumed to be the largest or longest mountain chain on the planet. Spin that satellite map, and you won't spot anything quite so conspicuous. It is a surprise to find, then, that the Asian range is only the sixth longest. Boss of the bunch is the Andes. At 7,000km (almost 4,350 miles), the South American range stretches two and a half times the distance. This is followed by the Southern Great Escarpment in Africa, the Rocky Mountains in North America, the Transantarctic range at the foot of the world and the Great Dividing Range in Australia. The Himalayas stand out for their sustained elevation, but they are nowhere near the most geographically expansive range on Earth.

All of these features are dwarfed by another parade of mountains, rarely glimpsed by the unaided human eye. The Mid-Atlantic Ridge is a vast submarine range whose location is handily given away by its name. This inundated chain could eat the Andes and Himalayas for breakfast. At around 16,000km (10,000 miles), it's longer than the pair combined. The southern end curls round into the Indian Ocean, connecting with a further undersea range. Were the world's oceans to disappear, an extreme mountaineer would find 40,000km (approximately 25,000 miles) of linked chains to tackle. Most of the Mid-Atlantic Ridge is deep below the waves, but it can be glimpsed in Iceland. It also underwrites a handful of Atlantic islands including the Azores and St Helena. Who knew that Napoleon was exiled to the world's longest mountain chain?

The Sahara is the world's biggest desert

What do you imagine when you see the word 'desert'? Wind-whipped sand dunes and a caravan of camels marching toward the setting sun? Perhaps a lone palm tree indicating an oasis in the distance? I just tried an Internet image search. Almost all the top 50 results showed some combination of these stereotypes*. Deserts are often sandy and, yes, camels do sometimes live in them. But there is much more variety among deserts than Lawrence of Arabia enthusiasts might credit.

In its simplest definition, a desert is a piece of land that doesn't see much precipitation (I would say 'rain', but the definition also includes snow, mist and fog). Few plants can grow. Few animals can survive. All deserts are harsh environments for life, but they need not be sandy. Large areas of the Arctic and Antarctic are considered deserts, for example. These icy wastes are half as big again as the Sahara – often cited as the world's largest desert.

In fact, only about one-fifth of the world's deserts are sandy, yellow and camel-prone. Some, like the Mojave in the USA, present hard-packed soils with a pebble-strewn topping. Others have various types of rock at the surface. The Painted Desert of Arizona comes in a disarming range of hues thanks to the iron and manganese compounds that permeate its rock. Egypt boasts both a white desert and a black desert, whose distinctive shades are caused respectively by chalk formations and volcanic deposits. Some deserts

---

* FOOTNOTE: And a blancmange. I'm guessing someone with good search-engine optimization doesn't know how to spell dessert.

are formed from gleaming white expanses of salt and other minerals left behind by evaporation from vanished lakes. The world's largest is Salar de Uyuni in Bolivia, roughly the size of Jamaica. The desert will be familiar to anyone who's seen *Star Wars: The Last Jedi* (2017), where – masquerading as the mineral planet Crait – it proves a memorable setting for the climactic battle scenes. The red undersoil and Jedi stronghold are pure fiction, though.

The driest desert on Earth is the Atacama in Chile. Some parts of the desert have yet to receive their first recorded hint of precipitation. No plants grow in these ultra-arid pockets; no animal but humans can intrude for long. Even so, the soils contain a variety of bacteria, giving hope that simple life may exist on equally arid parts of Mars.

The Nile is the world's longest river

How hard can it be to measure a river? You simply follow the waters from source to sea and calculate the distance. Unfortunately, it's not that simple. You can't pace it out along one of the banks. Rivers can meander wildly, so one bank may end up covering many more miles than the other if it happens to favour the outside bend more often. No problem: we'll measure along the middle of the river. But what counts as the middle, when the width of a river can change vastly and non-uniformly over the seasons? What if the river breaks into rival channels, which dance around then merge again? Which distance do we take if the river passes through a lake – like Lake Victoria near the source of the Nile? If you want to see how complex it can get, take a look at the Amazon south of Macapá.

The quibbles continue. What counts as the source? Any river is fed by numerous streams and springs. It must be so, otherwise it would never get wider. As we trace a river inland from the sea, we have to make a choice about which of the contributing waterways we follow. At first this is easy. The main flow of the river is much wider and more voluminous than the tributaries that feed into it. But as we get deeper inland, the main river narrows, and its tributaries become of similar size. Which is now the Amazon, and which an unnamed tributary? Which of these waters is the Nile, and which a feeder stream?

The argument can get very subjective. Some authorities would count the source stream as the one from highest elevation. Others would celebrate the water that flows the greatest distance. Sometimes the most distant source is dry for large portions of the year, so is overlooked in favour of something closer but wetter. Yet another argument could be made for the water which starts furthest west, or south, or whichever compass direction the main thrust of the river flows away from. Even the mouth of a river can be disputed. Rivers that end in deltas or have several divergent paths can vary in length depending on which route you choose.

What does this mean for the titular statement? Is the Amazon the world's longest river, or is it the Nile? Truthfully, you could argue it either way. Different authorities do just that. Guinness World Records plumps for the Nile, the traditional answer that most of us learnt at school. Even so, it concedes the accolade is 'more a matter of definition than simple measurement'. If we try Wikipedia, meanwhile, the Amazon comes top at 6,992km (4,345 miles), beating the Nile by 139km (just over 86 miles). This distance includes the Pará estuary, which sits aloof from the main Amazonian channels, but is nevertheless connected. All we can say for sure is that the Amazon is by far the world's largest river by volume, whichever route definition is used.

Most of the world's trees are in the Amazon

While we're in the area, let's take a moment to appreciate the Amazon Rainforest. It is truly immense. The South American feature (and 'feature' hardly seems a sufficient word) covers 5.5 million sq. km (2.1 million sq. miles). If it were a country, it would be the seventh largest in the world, much bigger than India, for example. It is filled with life like no other rainforest. Some 1,300 species of bird live here – about the same as China whose vast territory contains many more habitats. An estimated 2.5 million species of insect buzz and crawl beneath the canopy. Nobody has counted every tree, but the Amazon is estimated to contain some 390 billion individuals, of 16,000 species. Every person on the planet could lay claim to more than 50 trees. It's that big.

Even so, this is not the largest collection of trees on the planet. To find that, you have to head to the far north. The Boreal Forest, also known as the Taiga, is a band of trees that straddles the globe. This mostly coniferous woodland covers much of Canada and Alaska, northern Russia and Scandinavia. These are the lands of the spruce, larch and pine. The Taiga is not usually considered as a single forest. Rather, it is a *biome* – a distinct biological community of trees, other plants and animals that have evolved to thrive in a shared environment, in this case the Arctic and near-Arctic. Nevertheless, the Taiga comprises about 29 per cent of the world's forest cover. Estimates vary, but it seems about twice as many trees live in these boreal forests as in the Amazon.

For all its natural wonders, the Amazon is also home to a very surprising record-breaker. The Amazon Tall Tower Observatory is South America's tallest structure. At 325m (1,066ft), it's taller than the Eiffel Tower. Just let that sink in. One of the least-visited regions on the planet, surrounded by dense forest canopy, and 150km (just over 93 miles) from the nearest town is also home to a structure that would look down on any European landmark. The Amazon has no end of wonders, both natural and artificial.

Other myths and misnomers

Democratic Republic of ... : There's an old adage that if a country feels the need to append the words 'Democratic Republic' to its name, then it is probably neither democratic nor a republic. The former East Germany, for example, was officially styled the German Democratic Republic, despite a fierce appetite for communism. A current example, forever in the news, is the Democratic People's Republic of Korea – better known as North Korea. On paper, North Korea is a democracy, with multiple parties contesting elections every four to five years. But the elections are a charade. All candidates are ultimately members of the Democratic Front for the Reunification of the Fatherland, under the leadership of an hereditary dictator. Dissent is forbidden on pain of death. The Democratic Republic of the Congo hasn't fared much better. Civil war and corruption mark much of the east African nation's history since independence. The first free elections for four decades were held in 2006. Ongoing issues, such as the incumbent President's refusal to step down at the end of his term, mean that democracy in the country is tenuous at best. Other questionably named countries include the People's Democratic Republic of Algeria, the Federal Democratic Republic of Ethiopia and the one-party communist state of Laos, which is officially known as the Lao People's Democratic Republic.

Greenland: Of all the countries on Earth, Greenland is the least likely to conjure images of sylvan glades and verdant forests. Three-quarters of this land is covered in dense ice sheet with no vegetation. The misleading name is attributed to early Viking settler Eric the Red (these were hyperchromatic times). Living there in exile, he dubbed his new home Greenland in the hope of attracting fellow colonists. Few fell for this duplicitous PR exercise. Even today, the permanent population is just 56,000.

Las Vegas: The largest city in Nevada is world-famous for its casinos and shotgun weddings. Very little of the action is technically in Las Vegas, however. All those glowing signs, roulette wheels and shambolic nuptials really take place in the town of Paradise, just south of the city's borders. Paradise, otherwise known as the Las Vegas Strip, is an 'unincorporated town', meaning it is not restricted by the same laws and taxation regimes as regular towns. Hence its success as a freewheeling gambling den. If you ever get up to mischief in the town and try to silence the witnesses with the old line: 'What happens in Vegas, stays in Vegas,' then be careful you're not undermined on this technicality.

Lines of longitude and latitude: As a child, somebody convinced me that the horizontal and vertical lines on a globe were genuine features of the Earth. I thought they'd been painted or scored onto the ground as an

aid for navigators. For years, I believed that the planet had a mesh. While this is clearly not the case, there are places where lines of longitude or latitude have been marked. The most famous is the US-Canada border, much of which follows the 49th parallel (the circle of latitude 49°N of the equator). This is not only a notional line on a map. It has been gouged and chopped into the landscape, the full breadth of the continent. This great slash extends some 9,000km (5,592 miles) across the most rugged terrain. Check it out on a satellite map. No matter where you zoom in – forest, plains, mountains – there is the line, kept clear by the International Boundary Commission to a standard width of 6m (20ft). Any maths teachers reading this might like to set their class a problem in geometry. If the Commission were to mark out the full grid of my childhood misconception – that is every line of longitude and latitude at 1-degree intervals – how many kilometres would they have to cover?

Magma versus lava: The two words are often used as interchangeable alternatives for molten rock. There is a difference, and it's largely one of location. Magma, from the Greek phrase for 'thick unguent', is the correct word to use if we're talking about molten rock that is still within the Earth. Once geological forces have pushed it up to the surface, it should be called lava, a word that probably comes from the Latin for 'flow'.

The New World: This epithet for the Americas makes sense in the context of European exploration and conquest, which is to say the context in which it was coined by Amerigo Vespucci. From a grander historical view, though, the term feels a bit lame. The so-called New World was settled some 10,000–20,000 years ago by humans migrating across a land bridge between Siberia and Alaska. Admittedly, that's more recent than the 40,000 years since people first made it to 'Old World' Europe. But when we're talking about the sweep of aeons, 'old' and 'new' seem like quaint labels.

Pakistan: Most of the 'stans', like Tajikistan and Uzbekistan, are named after the people who settled there. Pakistan has an altogether more unusual, and recent, etymology. The word was first coined (as Pakstan) in 1933 by Choudhry Rahmat Ali. Ali was campaigning for the region's independence, which eventually happened in 1947. His choice of name was both an acronym and a pun. It is made up of key letters from the five constituent regions: **P**unjab, **A**fghania, **K**ashmir, **S**indh and Baluchi**stan**. Pakstan also means 'land of the pure' in Urdu. On independence, the 'i' was added to aid pronunciation. It remains the only recognized state to be created in the name of Islam.

Polar bears and penguins: It must be among the most common mistakes in cartoons and children's books: penguins and polar bears living happily together in snowy bliss. In the real world, polar bears are confined to the Arctic while penguins live in the Antarctic (as well as other parts of the Southern Hemisphere). They have never met in the wild. Beware, though, of how you phrase this distinction. It's often said that 'polar bears live at the North Pole while penguins live at the South Pole'. This is not true. Very few, if any, polar bears will reach the actual pole. Although it's always covered in sea ice, the pole is far from the main hunting grounds around the Arctic coasts. Likewise, penguins of the Antarctic tend to stick close to the sea. The pole is at least 1,500km (932 miles) from the ocean and is never enlivened by penguins.

Rare-earth metals: The neatness of the periodic table is marred by two semi-exiled rows, which float aloof at the bottom. These are the rare-earth elements, metals like cerium, terbium and europium that seldom troubled the chemistry classroom when I was growing up. These once-obscure materials are now in high demand. Almost all have found a role in the electronic gadgets that fill our homes and pockets. Despite the name, most rare earths aren't all that rare. Cerium, for example, is more abundant than copper in the Earth's crust. Even the rarest – lutetium and thulium – are 200 times more abundant than gold. It's just that rare-earth elements are rarely found in pure form. They don't cluster into ores and tend to gang up together. This makes them difficult to mine and separate. Dangerous, too, because they are often found alongside radioactive elements like uranium. Currently, about 85 per cent of the world's supply of rare earths comes from China.

The Seven Seas: An ancient phrase, used as a collective term for the world's impressive collection of salt water. The term is first noted in a Sumerian text more than 4,000 years old. The seven seas were matched to the seven classical 'planets' (the Sun, Mercury, Venus, the Moon, Mars, Jupiter and Saturn). In more recent times, it has been rationalized to fit seven large bodies of water: the Arctic, North Atlantic, South Atlantic, Indian, North Pacific, South Pacific and Antarctic Oceans. Taken literally, though, the number is woefully short of the mark. The world contains ten times as many seas as suggested by the idiom.

Swaziland: An African country that no longer exists. In April 2018, King Mswati announced that the nation would henceforth be known as the Kingdom of eSwatini. He rules as an absolute monarch, so can do this kind of thing. If you ignore the 'Kingdom' bit, then eSwatini is the world's only country to not begin with a capital letter – worth storing in your brain as it's sure to come up in a pub quiz, or a future edition of Trivial Pursuit.

The United Nations: At the time of writing, the United Nations is formed of 193-member states. They are not always united. In 1990, founding UN member Iraq went to war with fellow founding members the USA, UK, Saudi Arabia and France, after Iraq invaded and occupied long-standing member Kuwait. India (founder member) and Pakistan (1947) have traded bullets on several occasions. The Soviet invasion of Afghanistan in 1979 is yet another of many examples. Unity among the United Nations is an aspiration, not a circumstance.

Nor are all nations eligible to join the United Nations. The UN is a collection of sovereign states occupying defined territories. While 'nation' and 'state' are often used synonymously, there is a distinction. A nation is a group of people with a shared descent, culture and/or language. A state refers to a territory under one government. Nations are cultural or social collectives, while states are political. The two often coincide, but not always. A common example is the Jewish people who long existed as a nation without a state, until the formation of Israel in 1948. Among dozens of current examples, we might list the Tamils of South Asia, the Catalans and Basques of Spain, the Kurds of the Middle East, the Maori of New Zealand and the widespread Romani people. All are nations but are not eligible to join the United Nations. They lack sovereignty over a state. The United Nations is a lovely name, but more accurately described as the Disunited Nation-States.

Are you pronouncing it wrong?

Antipodes: In Britain, and the wider west, 'the Antipodes' is commonly used as a synonym for Australia and New Zealand. The term has a much wider meaning. It refers to any points (or regions) that lie directly opposite one another on the globe. London's antipode, as it happens, is in neither Australia nor New Zealand, but in the open Pacific Ocean. The word is pronounced 'antip-o-dees', rather than 'anti-podes'.

Archipelago: A cluster or chain of islands. The eye immediately alights on the 'arch-' and tempts the brain into reading this as 'arch-i-pel-a-go'. But the first syllable is derived from the Greek word *arkhi*, meaning 'chief'. That being the case, the modern word should be pronounced 'ark-i-PEL-e-goh'.

Basalt: The hard, igneous rock tends to be pronounced 'bass-alt' in the UK and 'buh-salt' across the Atlantic.

Belarus: This east-European country is sandwiched between Poland and Russia. The emphasis goes on the 'rus' bit, so we have 'bela-ROOZ'.

Eyjafjallajökull: The Icelandic glacier under which a volcano erupted in 2010, causing chaos to air traffic in northern Europe. Many at the time struggled to pronounce this unfamiliar run of syllables. When in doubt, see what the BBC's Pronunciation Unit has to say. Its suggested anglicization is 'AY-uh-fyat-luh-YOE-kuutl (-uh)', with the 'Ay' as in 'day', 'oe' as in French 'coeur' and 'uu' as in 'boot'.

Fjord: Another Norse word that makes an unnatural (to English-speakers) pairing of an 'f' and a 'j'. These inlets are pronounced as 'f-yords'.

Gneiss: A coarse-grained igneous rock, usually pale with bands and sparkly bits (as a geologist wouldn't say). Indeed, the word comes from the old German for 'spark'. The 'G' is silent, giving the word a pronunciation that is literally 'nice'.

Guinea-Bissau: This west-African nation has double potential to trip up the unwary. The first part is pronounced just as in 'guinea pig' (even though guinea pigs are not from Guinea, nor are they pigs). Bissau – also the name of the capital city – is pronounced 'biss-sowh'.

Isthmus: A narrow strip of land connecting two larger areas. Historically, the word was pronounced with a full-on flourish of that central 'th', as in is-th-mus. As that requires moderate lingual gymnastics, the term is often simplified to 'ist-mus'. This has the advantage of a near-rhyme with Christmas, for anyone composing outlandish carols.

Lesotho: A rare enclave country, Lesotho is entirely surrounded by South Africa. Its name is usually anglicized to 'Luh-soo-too', and not 'Luh-soth-o'.

Loess: A wind-blown dust and silt that covers about 10 per cent of the Earth's surface. The word is German in origin, originally written as löß. If you've got the oral dexterity to curl out that umlaut, then you have the best pronunciation of loess. If not, then go for 'lerss' as the next best thing. 'Low-ess' has become an acceptable pronunciation, but it is something of a stretch from the original form.

Magellan: Almost-round-the-world sailor Ferdinand Magellan is one of the great names from the Age of Discovery. How to say that great name is open to debate. It's either 'Ma-ghel-an', with a hard 'g', or 'Ma-jell-an', with a softer, jelly-like sound. Neither is incorrect. The former is favoured in Britain, the latter in the USA.

Pumice: This volcanic rock is pronounced as in 'pumpkin', and not as in 'puma'.

Let's start a new wave of false facts

Having debunked dozens of established myths, we need to create some new ones to replace them.

Gerardus Mercator, deviser of the famous map projection, was actually a flat-Earther. He developed his mapping technique as a way of proving that the Earth is not curved.

The Australian tectonic plate is being pushed in contrary directions by its neighbours. As a result, the whole plate is rotating anticlockwise by half a degree per year. In a few centuries, Australia will appear upside down on the map and Tasmania will become part of Indonesia.

The native islanders of Hawaii once practiced surfboarding on lava flows. The well-known surfer phrase 'to wipeout', meaning to be knocked off the board, originates from this dangerous sport, pioneered on the Wia Pouta volcano.

Researchers in China have found a way to print crude oil using a 3-D printer, meaning we need never fear a shortage again.

By law, the silhouette of Ferdinand Magellan must appear on the flag of Portugal. His likeness fills much of the right-hand portion of the flag in the same red hue as the background. Hence, it is invisible to the naked eye.

Alaska looks huge on the map, but it's really no bigger than Wales. The illusion is a side-effect of projecting the curved surface onto a 2-D map.

Despite its name, the G20 group of affluent nations comprises only 19 countries. The 20th is the fictional land of Figmentania. The fake nation, represented by an inflatable doll, only takes a seat during meetings if there would otherwise be 13 people at the table – an omen of ill luck.

Until a Papal Bull of 1373, the Earth was universally known as Terry.

Index

Abuja 8, 103
Afghanistan 28
Africa 8, 124
age of Earth 12–15
airports 19, 66
Alaska 76, 123, 137,
    155
Alps 138
Amazon 143–4, 145–6
Americas 56, 116–18
Amundsen, Roald 42
Andes 140
Antarctica 32, 33,
    36, 42, 47, 90, 109,
    124, 141, 150
antipodes 152
archipelago 152
Arctic 150
Arizona 141
ash clouds 66–7, 71–2
Astana 104
astronauts 8
Atlantis 128
atmosphere, radiation
    protection 22, 93–4
Australasia 120
Australia 32–3, 100,
    103, 124, 154
Austria 108–9

bacteria 97
Bahamas 118
Balboa, Vasco Núñez
    de 51
Bangladesh 37
basalt 152
Belarus 152
Bermuda 101, 118
Bir Tawil 36
Bolivia 142
borders 36, 108–9,
    112
Boreal Forest 145
boreholes 49
Brazil 103, 124
Britain 125–7
British Overseas
    Territories 38
buffer zones 38, 108

Cairo 105
calderas 69, 72, 74
Cambodia 44–5
Canada 149
cancer 22
capital cities 8, 102–5,
    106–7
carbon dioxide 88–90
Cardiff 121
Caribbean 113, 115,
    118
Caucasus mountains
    138
caves 45
Challenger Deep 46
Chatham Islands 28
Chicago 124
Chile 142
China 28, 100, 150
chlorofluorocarbons
    (CFCs) 93–4
circumnavigation
    50–3
cities
    capitals 8, 102–5,
        106–7
    lost 44
    oldest 111
city states 107
climate change 8, 86,
    87–92, 93–4
Columbus,
    Christopher 54–6
compasses 18–19, 22
condominiums 109
continents 32–3,
    124
core of the Earth 20,
    48–9, 77
countries
    age of 110–13
    definition 36
    names 133
    new 105
crust of the Earth
    77–8
Cuba 118
Cyprus 38
Czech Republic 123

Dahala Khagrabari 37
democracies 147
Democratic Republic
    of the Congo 147
Denmark 118, 119
deserts 141–2
Dominican Republic
    118

earthquakes 74, 75–6
east 16, 120
Ecuador 137
Edinburgh 121
Egypt 105, 120, 141
Egyptians, ancient 16
El Dorado 129
enclaves 37, 39
England 125
equator 35, 63
Equatorial Guinea 105
Eratosthenes 54, 56
Erikson, Leif 56
Europe 123, 138
Everest 8, 136–8
exploration 42–7
Eyjafjallajökull 66–7,
    152

false facts 154–5
Faroe Islands 118, 119
Finland 118–19
fjords 153
flag shapes 39, 100–1
flat-Earthers 54–5,
    57–61, 154
flint 80–1
Florida 8, 122–3, 124
forests 44, 145–6
fossil fuels 79–80, 88
fossils 12–13
France 28, 106, 113

G20 nations 155
gas 79
geology 13, 14–15
Germany 102, 108–9,
    111, 147
geysers 71
global warming see

climate change
gneiss 153
gold 77–8, 79
GPS 17, 60
Great Britain 121,
    125–6
Greeks, ancient 54
greenhouse gases 88
Greenland 32, 33,
    90–1, 118, 119,
    132, 147
Greenwich Meridian
    24
Guatemala 44, 101
Guinea-Bissau 153
Gulf States 112, 120

Haití 118
Hawaii 69, 110, 137,
    154
Himalayas 136,
    139–40
Holland 114–15
Hooke, Robert 13
hotspots 69, 95–6
Hughes, 'Mad' Mike
    57–8
Hutton, James 13
hydrothermal vents
    95–7

ice ages 84–6
Iceland 118, 119, 140
India 28, 37, 100,
    130, 131
Indonesia 50, 105
International Date
    Line 123
Iran 28, 120
Iraq 112, 120
Ireland 111, 126, 127
iron 20, 48
Island of California 130
islands 32–3, 109,
    115, 118
Isle of Man 101, 126
Israel 36, 111
Istanbul 124
isthmus 153

Italy 111
Ivory Coast 105

Kaliningrad Oblast 37
Kazakhstan 104, 105
Kepler, Johannes 12

Lagos 8, 103
Lake Constance 108–9
lakes, salt 31
Las Vegas 148
latitude 148–9
lava 20, 49, 67, 69,
    149, 154
Lemuria 130–1
Lesotho 8, 39, 153
Liberia 101
Libya 101
life 95–6
lightning 82–3
loess 153
London 106, 124
longitude 148–9

Madagascar 130, 131
Magellan, Ferdinand
    50–3, 153, 155
magma 49, 149
magnetic field 18–22,
    49
Maine 8, 123
mantle 48–9
maps 16–17, 32, 46–7,
    54, 121–3, 130–1,
    154
Mariana Trench 46
Marshall Islands 101
Maseru 8
Melanesia 120
meridians 24
metals, rare-earth
    80–1, 150
Mexico 44, 116–18
Micronesia 101, 105,
    120
Mid-Atlantic Ridge 140
Middle East 111–12,
    120
mining 77–8, 79–81
moment magnitude
    scale (MMS) 75–6
mountains 136–8,
    139–40

Mountains of Kong
    and Moon 131
Mozambique 101
Myanmar 103, 105

Napoleon 114, 140
nations 151
navigation 16, 22
Naypyidaw 103
Nepal 28, 101, 136
Netherlands 107,
    114–15, 125
New Guinea 120
'New World' 110–13,
    149
New Zealand 28, 120
Newton, Isaac 12, 63
Nigeria 8, 103, 105
Nile 143–4
Nordic countries
    118–19
north 16
North Atlantic Gyre 31
North Korea 28, 74,
    147
North Pole 16, 18–23,
    42
Northern Cyprus 38
Northern Ireland 126
Norway 118, 119

Oceania 120
oceans 30–1, 46–7,
    69, 90, 95–7
oil 155
oil reserves 79–80
orbit of the Earth
    34–5
orientation 16
ozone layer 8, 93–4

Pacific 46, 51
Pakistan 103, 149–50
Palau 105
Palestine 36
Panama 51, 116
Paris 106
penguins 150
Pheasant Island 109
photosynthesis 95, 97
planets 95
plate tectonics 8, 49,
    131, 139–40, 154

polar bears 150
Pole Star 16
Polynesia 120
Portugal 103, 155
Prague 123
Prime Meridian 24,
    25, 28
pronunciation 152–3
Puerto Rico 38, 118
pumice 153

radiometric dating
    14–15
rainforests 44, 145–6
relgion 15
resource depletion
    79–81
Richter scale 75–6
'Ring of Fire' 67, 76
Rio de Janeiro 103
rivers 143–4
rock formation 13, 20
rotation of the Earth 23
Russia 37, 100, 124,
    138

Saint Kitts and Nevis
    113
San Andreas fault 76
Sandy Island 131
Santorini 69
Sargasso Sea 31
satellites 22, 43–4,
    59, 60
satnavs 17
Saudi Arabia 112, 120
Scandinavia 118
sea levels 47, 85, 91
Sea of Galilee 31
seas 30–1, 150–1
seasons 34–5
sediments 13
seismic waves 49,
    75–6
shape of Earth 62–3
snow 91, 139
Somaliland 38
sonar 46
south 16
South America 124,
    145–6
South Korea 28
South Pole 18, 42

sovereign states 151
Sri Lanka 28, 105
Sun as requirement for
    life 95
sunburn 22
Svalbard 122
Swaziland 151
Sweden 118, 119
Switzerland 39, 101,
    108–9

Taiga 145
Taiwan 36
Tanzania 105
temperature
    climate change 90
    Earth's core 48
territory, ownership
    108–9
Thule 132
tilt of the Earth 35
time zones 24–9
trees 145–6
tsunamis 76
Turkey 38, 120
Turks and Caicos
    islands 118

United Kingdom 36,
    100, 110, 125–7
United Nations (UN)
    36, 94, 151
up 16–17
uranium 14, 150
USA 8, 70–4, 76, 101,
    110, 123–4, 125, 149
Ussher, James, Rev 12

Vatican City 39, 101,
    107
volcanoes 49, 66–9,
    70–4, 154

Wales 36
weather extremes
    91–2
west 17
winter 34–5

Yellowstone National
    Park 69, 70–4

zircon 14–15

157

Other titles in the series

Everything You Know About
London is Wrong
9781849943604

Everything You Know About
Science is Wrong
9781849944021